Table of Contents

God's Answers To Heal Your Deep Hurts

FOREWORD

By Morris Cerullo

The fact that you're reading this book tells me you've been hurt.

You may say, "No, I picked up this book to learn how to deal with someone else's problem..."

But I believe God has led you to pick up this book for a reason. When you decided to open these pages, God already had decided to minister to your deep hurts, and your inner pain.

It's OK. Everyone's been hurt before. If you've never been hurt, you've never been alive.

God has led me to write this book because He wants you to lay your cares upon Him.

If anyone was ever hurt by the scorn of man...

If anyone was ever hurt by the rejection of those they loved...

If anyone was ever hurt by the pain of a child dying...

If anyone was ever hurt by finding out that someone he loved hated him...

It was Jesus.

Listen to what Isaiah says about Jesus:

For he shall grow up before him as a tender plant, and as a root out of a dry ground: he hath no form nor comeliness; and when we shall see him, there is no beauty that we should desire him. He is despised and rejected of men; a man of sorrows, and acquainted with grief: and we hid as it were our faces from him; he was despised, and we esteemed him not. Surely he hath borne our griefs, and carried our sorrows: yet we did esteem him stricken, smitten of God, and afflicted.

Isaiah 53:2-4

Did you read that?

Jesus is a MAN OF SORROWS! He is despised. He is rejected...

He is a man of sorrows Who is acquainted with grief!

Do you hurt?

Jesus understands.

Is there a pain deep in your gut that just seems to sit there like a lead weight? A pain so deep that it's a dull throb all day long? A pain so deep that the enemy has been whispering in your ear that maybe it would be better if you weren't here at all?

Jesus understands...

He's been there.

He's acquainted with your grief, your dull, throbbing pain...

He's lived in your sorrow.

> *These things I have spoken unto you, that in me ye might have peace. In the world ye shall have tribulation: but be of good cheer; I have overcome the world.*
>
> John 16:33

Jesus has walked in your shoes and has borne your burden.

He's been rejected. He's been ridiculed. He's been humiliated. He's been thrown out. Those who were closest to Him turned their backs on Him and denied even knowing him.

But don't fear...

Don't worry...

JESUS HAS OVERCOME THE WORLD!

Jesus has lived in your pain AND HE HAS CONQUERED IT!

Don't let your situation conquer you.

Jesus is waiting to take your burden off your shoulders. He is standing ready to lift your pain and relieve your hurt.

Picking up this book was your first step. God has sent His anointing to set you free.

As you read, be careful to absorb every word.

You may want to read this book more slowly than you would another book.

You don't want to miss a single word.

If you find yourself skimming over parts, stop yourself, back up, and read again.

This book is built, line upon line, precept upon precept, to reach deep into your heart and allow the Holy Ghost to lift the burden of your pain.

This book is *my* heart talking to *your* heart.

Over my more than 58 years of ministry, God has revealed the truths in this book to my heart.

Now I want to share them with you and pour them into your spirit.

You may want to close the door, take the phone off the hook, and sit in a comfortable chair as you read on.

God has prepared a victory for you over your hurt, your pain.

I love you more than words can say. My prayer is that this book will be an instrument in God's hands to set you free!

Your friend,
God's servant,

Morris Cerullo

GOD WANTS YOU TO EXPERIENCE TOTAL WHOLENESS...SPIRIT...SOUL...BODY!

God wants to heal your deep hurts, the wounds, the scars in your life and bring you into a new level of victory and power where you are 100 percent WHOLE...spirit...soul...and body!

The Body of Christ is hurting! God has shown me that the Church is filled with wounded Christians. The Church is like an army marching out into battle with its soldiers battered...hurting...with gaping, open wounds.

Multitudes of Christians are carrying deep hurts from the past. Their spirits have been grievously wounded. On the surface they seem to be victorious...there are smiles on their faces...they are speaking words of faith and victory...they are ministering to the needs of others...yet, within their own spirits are deep, gaping wounds which have never been healed.

Many of those who have been wounded have tried to overlook or deny their hurts. They have tried to cover them up or hide them. Christians today are carrying deep hurts from the past, and yet they're not even aware of it.

GOD IS GOING TO BRING YOU TO A NEW POSITION OF TOTAL WHOLENESS!

There is not one person alive today who has not been hurt at some time in their life. Ninety-nine percent of Christians have been hurt at some time within the Church...church splits...trust betrayed by a pastor or other church members...misunderstandings...gossip and slander. Satan is using these hurts to weaken the Church and bring strife and division by causing Christians who have been hurt to build walls of bitterness, resentment and unforgiveness against other members within the Body.

If you allow him, Satan will use the past hurts in your life to hinder you from walking in the freedom and power Christ has made possible for you.

He will use them to weaken you where you feel worn out...physically, spiritually and mentally...burned out and defeated.

> *And let us not be weary in well doing: for in due season*
> *we shall reap, if we faint not.*
>
> Galatians 6:9

Don't listen to Satan's lie that it is not God's will to heal you! God's plan for his people has always been TOTAL WHOLENESS.

A time of healing and restoration is coming to the Body of Christ! Just as God promised Israel, His promise to us today is:

> *For I will restore health unto thee, and I will heal thee*
> *of thy wounds, saith the Lord!*
>
> Jeremiah 30:17

I have taught for years in the Schools Of Ministry and around the world that the Church of Jesus Christ is not going to remain in a weakened, anemic condition.

We are going to be raptured in a greater demonstrative power than the Early Church was born in!

By His Spirit, God is going to sweep through the Body of Christ in a powerful manifestation of healing and restoration.

Members of the Body of Christ who have been wounded in battle...who are battle-torn and weary, are going to rise up in a new strength.

Many who have been crippled and bound by pain and disease are going to rise up off their beds of affliction...healed and set free by the power of God!

God is not only going to heal the deep hurts that are in our lives; He is going to use us to help heal and bind up the wo;unds of other members within the Body of Christ.

Before we can go forward in the strength, power and authority God has planned and ordained for us in this end-time hour, we must begin to bind up the wounds of those who have been battered and broken.

Christ wants His Body to be whole in every way.

We are to be God's "healing center," where those who are crippled in spirit: brokenhearted, broken emotionally, and battered, can come and be made WHOLE!

As the Body of Christ, we have the same purpose Christ had when He began His ministry.

Jesus stood in the synagogue of His hometown and declared His purpose from the prophecies concerning Himself as the promised Messiah.

He declared:

The Spirit of the Lord is upon me, because he hath

11

anointed me to preach the gospel to the poor; he hath sent me to heal the brokenhearted, to preach deliverance to the captives, and recovering of sight to the blind, to set at liberty them that are bruised, To preach the acceptable year of the Lord.

Luke 4:18-19

Jesus said He was sent to heal those who were "brokenhearted" and to set free those who were "bruised."

You and I have been given the same purpose.

We have been anointed with the Holy Spirit and power, and sent forth to heal those who have been crushed-who are bruised, broken and bleeding from deep hurts-by the problems, trials and tragedies they have experienced in their lives.

IT IS TIME FOR US TO POUR IN THE OIL AND THE WINE!

God's promise to us today is:

For I will restore health unto thee, and I will heal thee of thy wounds, saith the Lord.

Jeremiah 30:17

THE HURTS OF YOUR PAST DO NOT NEED TO DEFEAT OR DESTROY YOU!

God desires to heal the deep wounds in our lives, and bring the Body of Christ into a position of strength.

He wants to heal our memories, and free us from the pain and guilt of the past.

He wants to bring you to a position of new spiritual freedom and TOTAL WHOLENESS.

Regardless of how deeply you may have been wounded or how broken and battered you may feel, God will heal you of those deep hurts and release you from the past.

God has not planned any defeats for you! There is absolutely NOTHING Satan can bring into your life that can defeat you NOTHING!

Say this aloud: "There is no problem, no circumstance, no trial, no temptation, no test Satan can bring into my life that can defeat me!" The hurts of your past do not have to defeat or destroy you, regardless of how deep the wounds may be.

It is HOW YOU REACT AND RESPOND to those hurts that can destroy you.

We must accept the fact that, in this life, we will sometimes be mistreated.

There are Christians today who think that as long as they are serving God and are walking in obedience to Him, they are somehow exempt from pain, infirmities, and hurts most people experience.

Christians ARE NOT EXEMPT from pain and the deep hurts in this life! To walk in victory, we must realize that there will be times in our lives when we will be misjudged and misunderstood.

There will be times when we will do good and instead of being appreciated, we will be mistreated by others.

Jesus warned, *"In the world ye shall have tribulation: but be of good cheer; I have overcome the world"* (John 16:33).

He said,

> *Ye Shall be hated of all men for my name's sake.*
> Matthew 10:22

The apostle Paul told Timothy, *"All that will live godly in Christ Jesus shall suffer persecution"* (II Timothy 3:12).

He told the Corinthians:

> *We are troubled on every side, yet not distressed; we are perplexed, but not in despair; Persecuted, but not forsaken; cast down, but not destroyed.*
> II Corinthians 4:8-9

Throughout his lifetime Paul experienced much pain and suffering.

He knew the pain of persecution, afflictions, beatings, imprisonment and betrayal by false brethren. (II Corinthians 11:24-28)

He endured many deep hurts in the course of his life, yet they did not overwhelm or defeat him because he knew how to react to them.

The trials, tests, and sufferings he experienced did not discourage or weaken him, but actually caused him to grow stronger.

NOTHING Satan brings into your life can defeat you.

Friend, THE DEVIL IS A LIAR!

Regardless of how deeply you may have been hurt in the past or may be hurting today, those hurts cannot overwhelm or defeat you when you know the secret to overcoming them.

You may have been abused or mistreated by a family member...falsely accused...misjudged, misrepresented or slandered by a brother or sister in the Lord...unfairly treated by an employer... abandoned or betrayed by a close friend or loved one.

None of these hurts can weaken or destroy you as long as you refuse to hold onto them or allow a ROOT OF BITTERNESS to take hold in your life.

ARE YOU CHAINED TO HURTS OF THE PAST?

One of the reasons why many Christians are not walking in the power and freedom God intended for them as sons of the living God, is because they are still carrying and holding onto the hurts of the past.

They are chained to their hurts and to those who have hurt them through bitterness, resentment, and unforgiveness.

Feelings of anger, self-pity, bitterness, resentment, and even hate will try to rise up within us after we have been hurt, and will try to control us if we allow them to.

We try to shut out the pain, to forget the memory and put it out of our minds once and for all, but Satan will come to stir it up and will try to use the hurts to torment and keep us in a weakened position.

There are times when we would like to forgive those who have hurt us, but the bitter feelings keep coming back and it seems we have no control over them.

15

Are you still carrying hurts from your past? Are there any hurts in your life which have never been healed?

You may think, "Brother Cerullo, you just don't know how deeply I was hurt. After what has been done to me, I can never forgive or forget how that person has hurt me."

It may be that you are still carrying hurts from your past which occured ten, twenty, thirty years ago, or more. You may not have seen the person who hurt you for years.

The one who hurt you may have died and been buried many years ago.

But, as long as you hold bitterness and unforgiveness in your heart toward the person who hurt you, you remain bound to them, and the wounds you suffered cannot be healed.

If you are one who has been deeply hurt, if you are carrying deep wounds which have never fully healed, or you know someone who is crushed and brokenhearted, the Word of God today is:

> *For I will restore health unto thee, and I will heal thee*
> *of thy wounds, saith the LORD...*
>
> Jeremiah 30:17

Regardless of how deeply we have been hurt in the past or may be hurt in the future, we do not have to become victims.

We do not have to be discouraged and defeated.

The hurts and events of the past that may haunt you and continue to play and replay in your mind can be healed and turned off.

Remember, the hurts of the past or those you will receive in your lifetime, cannot defeat or destroy you.

How you react and respond to those hurts is what will weaken and eventually destroy you!.

ALLOW GOD TO REVEAL AND HEAL ANY WOUNDS YOU MAY STILL BE CARRYING!

Seven strategies Satan will try to use to cause you to react to the hurts in your life will not only block the healing of the wounds, but will also keep you in a weakened position physically, spiritually, and mentally:

- Anger
- Withdrawal
- Self-pity
- Revenge
- Bitterness
- Unforgiveness
- Resentment

Uncovering the wounds and hurts in your life may be painful.

But, we cannot continue to overlook them, cover them up, or pretend they are not there.

God wants to bring healing and restoration to the Body of Christ.

He wants to bring us to a new position of strength! The Body of Christ today cannot be the "healing center" God intended it to be when we are still wounded and in a weakened state.

We cannot face the coming crises and destroy the powers of darkness in this end-time harvest when many within the Body of Christ are spiritually crippled, wounded, and discouraged, battle-worn, and defeated.

We must experience a healing touch from God to rise up and prepare for this end-time battle.

Only when we are healed and strengthened will we be able to open the doors of our churches and declare to the world, "We are in the healing business! Crippled and wounded people can come and find healing...new strength...TOTAL WHOLENESS...spirit...soul...body...here!"

GOD WANTS TO DO SOME SPIRITUAL SURGERY ON YOU!

God wants to heal the hurts and wounds in your life.

But, you must openly and honestly come before Him, and ask Him to expose any wounds which have not yet been healed in your life.

It may be that you are suffering deep hurts and emotional scars that you received in church relationships.

Another brother or sister in the Lord may have gossiped or offended you in some way.

It may be that you have shut that brother or sister who has hurt you out of your heart because of unforgiveness, or built walls of resentment, cutting off your relationship with them.

God desires to bring healing to your hurts and reconciliation into that relationship, whereby you are restored to your brother or sister in the Lord.

As long as there is bitterness, resentment, and unforgivness in relationships between members of the Body of Christ, there is DIVISION and we remain in a weakened condition! It may be that you are suffering deep hurts in your family relationships with a rebellious son or daughter or husband or wife who has been unfaithful.

You may feel the broken, crushed heart of a trust that has been betrayed in your marriage relationship.

You may feel the deep, deep pain of rejection by a mate who has divorced you or has informed you he or she wants a divorce.

God planned our homes to be a place where we could find love, acceptance, forgiveness, and spiritual nourishment. Yet, many have become a battleground! In Christian homes today there is a crisis of anger, rage, abuse, and secret violence behind closed doors.

It is sad to say, but true, that many children in Christian homes are growing up broken in spirit...their self-esteem battered...bitter...discouraged...wounded...and filled with despair.

Domestic violence in America is commonplace.

One of the best kept secrets in the American Church is the amount of violence occuring within church-going families.

It may be that you are still carrying hurts from your childhood...rejection by your parents...verbal abuse...sexual abuse...loss of self-esteem...a sense of never being accepted by your parents, nor living up to their standards.

You may be hurting because of some injustice you have experienced on your job.

Your employer may have verbally abused or mistreated you.

It may be that you have not been given the raise or salary that you feel is justly yours.

You may be carrying deep hurts you recieved through a deep personal loss...loss of a husband or wife, child, or family member through death...the loss of your health through a prolonged disease...the loss of a home through disaster or bankruptcy.

Whatever hurts you may be carrying from the past or may be suffering right now, don't be afraid to recognize them.

God wants to begin the healing process in your life today!

Allow God to expose those hurts so you can begin to receive healing and restoration in your life.

You are going to learn a powerful truth that is the key to total healing and TOTAL WHOLENESS, which will enable you to walk in greater strength and victory.

YOUR SPIRIT HAS BEEN SUPERNATURALLY EMPOWERED AND CHARGED BY GOD'S MIGHTY POWER!

There is no hurt too deep or no wound too great, that God cannot heal!

Right now you may be going through such pain and heartache that you feel you cannot possibly endure another moment.

You may have been hurt so deeply that you feel you will never be able to fully recover.

God is going to heal your wounds and restore you to a position of strength!

When we are hurt, not only are our emotions affected, but the hurt goes deep down into our SPIRITS...into our inner being.

Our spirits become grieved and wounded. If an individual is hurt repeatedly over a long period of time, his spirit will eventually become weakened and broken.

There are children and young people today who have been physically or verbally abused, neglected and rejected by their parents throughout their childhood.

They have experienced hurt after hurt until their spirit is crushed and broken.

They feel unloved and unwanted.

CHAPTER TWO

In some instances, they have actually been told they are unwanted.

In cases of verbal abuse, these children are continually humiliated and ridiculed until they develop such a low self-esteem, they give up and stop trying to accomplish anything.

Over and over they are attacked with cruel, vicious words until they believe what they are hearing.

Their parents have told them, "You're so clumsy! Why can't you do anything right?" Or, "You're so stupid. You will never amount to anything." "I wish you had never been born." The children's spirits were broken.

They are deeply wounded by rejection and lose self-esteem and self-worth.

A root of bitterness, anger, and resentment toward their parents begins to take hold in their lives and unless they receive God's healing touch, they carry those deep hurts and wounds into adulthood.

Some adults were sexually abused or molested as children by a parent, family member, or close family friend. Their spirits were wounded, crushed, and broken.

Those deep wounds have not been healed and they are still carrying them, buried deep within their spirits.

There are husbands and wives who have been verbally abused or physically battered by their mates until their spirits were broken.

Unlike the physical wounds which eventually heal, the deep wounds their spirits have received do not.

They try to shut out pain by withdrawing into themselves so they won't be hurt again, or they become filled with anger, bitterness, and resentment against their mates.

Eventually, their relationship is destroyed, often ending in further pain through separation and divorce.

When we came to Christ and accepted Him as our Savior, we were healed: totally and completely from the course of sin.

The power of sin was broken over us.

We were totally cleansed of all our sins, and God placed His Spirit within us.

We were healed of our sins.

Jesus paid the price on the cross.

The work has already been finished!

> *Surely he hath borne our griefs, and carried our sorrows: yet we did esteem him stricken, smitten of God, and afflicted. But he was wounded for our transgressions, he was bruised for our iniquities: the chastisement of our peace was upon him; and with his stripes we are healed.*
>
> Isaiah 53:4-5

But, even though we have been cleansed and set free from our sin, all of us have areas in our lives...wounds in our spirits...that are still painful and need the healing touch of God.

Jesus had already taken all our grief and sorrows upon Himself.

But, we must come to Him and allow Him to heal our wounded spirits.

Some have painful memories and need God to heal those memories, enabling them to break the chains of their past.

Many have been wounded deeply by others...friends... family members...husband or wife...co-workers...Christian brothers and sisters...and desperately need God's healing touch in their spirits.

We must have God's healing touch! If we hold onto those deep hurts, our spirits will remain in a weakened condition and we will be giving Satan an opportunity to sow seeds of anger, bitterness, self-pity, resentment, and unforgiveness, which will block God's healing in our lives, and will eventually destroy us if we allow it.

A STRONG SPIRIT WILL ENABLE A MAN TO OVERCOME HIS INFIRMITIES

As long as a Christian is wounded and broken in spirit, he cannot endure and overcome the trials, sickness, and adverse circumstances which come into his life.

If his spirit is in a weakened condition, he will not be able to fight off sickness and disease, and he will break physically.

However, when his spirit is strong and healthy, he will be able to stand victorious over the greatest trials and tribulations he may face.

When your spirit is strong, you will be able to endure and overcome sickness and disease! Look closely at Proverbs 18:14: *"The spirit of a man will sustain his infirmity; but a wounded spirit who can bear?"*

There is a powerful key to healing and TOTAL WHOLENESS in this Scripture, which enables you to walk in greater strength and victory! The spirit, soul, and body are very closely linked together.

When an individual's spirit is wounded or broken, he becomes discouraged and his heart and mind are filled with unbelief, worry, and stress.

As a result, his body is affected and he often begins to experience physical problems.

A great majority of health problems today are stress-related and stem from inability to cope with the pressures, problems, and tragedies we face.

It is also true that the physical condition of our bodies often affects our minds and spirits.

When an individual is suffering pain and disease in his body, many times he becomes depressed, and his spirit becomes filled with doubt and unbelief.

Our physical condition has caused our spirits to become weakened, and we are unable to reach out in faith for our healing.

In the natural world, our spirits enable our bodies to bear up under great trials and afflictions.

The Word says, "The spirit of a man will sustain his infirmity..." An individual who has a strong spirit can endure and survive some of the greatest tragedies and the worst possible afflictions.

Men and women have been known to endure and overcome tremendous personal losses...the loss of their entire family due to a major tragedy...paralysis of their entire body...severe pain due to debilitating disease...bankruptcy... but have overcome tremendous obstacles and severe handicaps in accomplishing their goals in life because their spirits and wills were strong.

On the other hand, some have faced less severe problems, afflictions, and diseases who have not been able to overcome or survive because they have a BROKEN SPIRIT.

Some have been hospitalized with bodily injuries or a sickness which others have survived, but they did not because their spirits had been broken and they had lost their will to live.

They were broken in spirit and just gave up.

When an individual has a broken spirit and has given up his will to live, there is very little doctors can do.

But Jesus came to heal the brokenhearted and to heal those who have been bruised and crushed.

He is the only one who can heal a broken spirit!

The human body, when it is weary, weakened, or afflicted, is supported by the spirit that sustains and enables the body to bear up and endure under affliction.

However, if the spirit is grieved, overwhelmed, weakened, or broken, the body has no resource to fall back upon and it succumbs to the pain and pressure.

The natural spirit that is within us is strong and can enable us to overcome a lifetime habit of drug or alcohol abuse, overeating, or other such things. We have been able to overcome seemingly insurmountable odds through the power of "positive thinking." Although, I believe in the power of positive thinking, I also believe it is limited to the natural realm.

The emphasis is upon one's ability...one's strength and mental power alone.

I focus upon God's supernatural ability, rather than one's ability.

YOUR SPIRIT IS STRENGTHENED BY HIS MIGHT!

Now, let us go deeper into the spiritual realm to look at the natural spirit that has been infused in us and empowered by the Spirit of God.

The "spirit" of man is the quality of life that God gives to us.

It is the part of us whereby we can communicate with God and worship him.

> *God is a Spirit: and they that worship Him must worship Him in sprit and in truth.*
>
> John 4:24

God *"...formeth the spirit of man within him"* (Zechariah 12:1).

When you accepted Christ as your Savior, He placed His Spirit within your spirit and you were born again.

Your spirit has been strengthened and empowered by God's divine Spirit! Paul told the Corinthians, *"Know ye not that ye are the temple of God, and that the Spirit of God dwelleth in you?"* (I Corinthians 3:16)

He said, *"But ye are not in the flesh, but in the Spirit, if so be that the Spirit of God dwell in you. Now if any man have not the Spirit of Christ, he is none of his"* (Romans 8:9).

Our spirits have been "quickened"...MADE ALIVE...by Christ, Who lives within us by His Spirit! The very life of Christ has been manifested within us.

We are no longer living our lives according to our "natural man" or "natural spirit," but according to His Spirit within us.

Do you realize what this means to you today?

Because of His Spirit that is living within you, you are MORE THAN ABLE to endure and overcome every trial... every circumstance...every sickness...every tragedy that may come into your life!

The Word says, *"the spirit of a man will sustain his infirmity."* If our natural spirit can enable us to endure and overcome our infirmities, think about how much more we are able to walk in total victory when our spirits have been infused and empowered by His Spirit!

By His Spirit living within you, your spirit is SUPERNATURALLY EMPOWERED! The life of Christ is flowing through you, and you are not only able to withstand every affliction, every sickness, and every trial that comes into your life, but you will be able to live in TOTAL WHOLENESS...SPIRIT...SOUL...BODY!

Paul prayed:

> *May He grant you out of the rich treasury of His glory to be strengthened and reinforced with mighty power in the inner man by the (Holy)Spirit(Himself)–indwelling your innermost being and personality.*
>
> Ephesians 3:16, AMP

In the King James version, this verse is translated *"...to be strengthened with might by His Spirit in the inner man"* (Ephesians 3:16).

Your spirit has been strengthened and reinforced by HIS MIGHTY POWER! Paul prayed that the Colossians would be

> *Strengthened with all might, according to His glorious power, unto all patience and longsuffering with joyfulness.*
>
> Colossians 1:11

Circle the word "might" in these verses.

It is translated from the Greek word "dunamis," which is the same miracle-working power that is in Jesus.

It refers to inherent ability and capability...the ability to perform anything!

Through His "MIGHT" — His "dunamis" miracle-working power that is in out spirits — we have the ability and capability to face every trial, carry any burden, overcome every obstacle, and face every challenge in His strength! In these prayers, Paul did not pray for physical or mental strength, but for the believers to be strengthened WITHIN THEIR SPIRIT...IN THE INNER MAN.

He prayed for SPIRITUAL STRENGTH...that their spirits would be endued with ALL MIGHT...the "dunamis" power of God.

Notice the measure of strength Paul prayed for them to receive, *"...according to the riches of His glory..."* (Ephesians 3:16) and, *"...according to His glorious power..."* (Colossians 1:11).

The spiritual strength that is available to us today is a measure, not according to our weaknesses, not according to our need, or even according to what we can think or comprehend, but according to the ABUNDANCE OF HIS GLORY...the "doxa" of God...all that God is and has.

We have access to an IMMEASURABLE...INEXHAUSTIBLE supply of His grace, love, mercy, and power that is existent in Him! The source of this strength and the means whereby our spirits are strengthened is BY HIS SPIRIT LIVING WITHIN US! God is able to do, *"...exceeding abundantly above all that we ask or think, according to the power that worketh in us"* (Ephesians 3:20).

Through the Holy Spirit that is within us, we are able to draw daily from God's IMMEASURABLE, INEXHAUSTIBLE supply and be strengthened with ALL MIGHT...His "dunamis" power within our spirits.

The purpose of this vast supply of spiritual strength is that we will be able to withstand the onslaught of the enemy, resist temptation, endure, be victorious in affliction and persecution, and do the mighty works of God! Paul told the Corinthians, *"For which cause we faint not; but though our outward man perish, yet the inward man is renewed day by day"* (II Corinthians 4:16).

Though our physical bodies are subject to weakness and decay, we are equipped and prepared to walk in God's dunamis power on a daily basis by His Spirit working within us.

"DUNAMIS": WE HAVE AN IMMEASURABLE, INEXHAUSTIBLE SUPPLY OF GOD'S POWER!

This IMMEASURABLE, INEXHAUSTIBLE supply of His strength is available to us, but we must draw upon it.

Just as our physical strength is dependent upon food and rest, our spiritual strength is dependent upon our daily drawing strength from God through prayer, waiting upon God...living in His presence...daily feeding upon the Word, and applying it to our lives.

The reason many Christians today are spiritually weak and unable to overcome the adverse circumstances of their lives and be victorious over the power of the enemy, is because they have failed to draw upon God's "dunamis" strength.

They have been walking according to their own natural strength, and their strength has been exhausted.

In this weakened condition, they have become vulnerable to the attacks of the enemy.

They are unable to resist or overcome the attacks of the enemy and have become wounded and battered.

Look at Proverbs 18:14 again:

The spirit of a man will sustain his infirmity; but a wounded spirit who can bear?

When a Christian's spirit has become wounded, overwhelmed, weakened, or broken, they are unable to bear up under the trials, burdens, and physical afflictions.

There is a sense of emptiness...a feeling that they are at the end of their strength.

They feel totally drained, dry, and unable to go on.

This is the reason that it is so important for Christians who are still carrying hurts from the past to allow God to heal their wounds and restore them to a new position of strength.

God's Spirit is LIVING within our spirits.

And by His Spirit within us, we can draw daily upon His IMMEASURABLE, INEXHAUSTIBLE SUPPLY of strength.

By His Spirit, our spirits are strengthened and empowered by His dunamis power. To have God's dunamis power manifested within your spirit so that you will be able to walk in this new dimension of power and victory, you must:

- Recognize the areas where you have become wounded in your spirit

- Allow God to heal you of your wounds

- Guard your spirit against becoming wounded

SIN WOUNDS AND WEAKENS OUR SPIRITS!

Let us look now at the major ways our spirits become wounded, weakened, overwhelmed, and broken.

Any time we yield to sin in our lives, our spirits are wounded...and as long as there is unconfessed sin in our lives, those wounds remain and will not heal.

When David had sinned, he cried out to God:

> *For mine iniquities are gone over mine head: as an heavy burden they are too heavy for me. My wounds stink and are corrupt because of my foolishness. I am troubled; I am bowed down greatly; I go mourning all the day long...I am feeble and sore broken: I have roared by reason of the disquietness of my heart.*
>
> Psalm 38:4-6, 8

We must be constantly on guard that we do not allow unconfessed sin to remain in our spirits.

Sin grievously wounds our spirit and brings guilt and suffering.

When we have sin in our lives that we have failed to gain victory over, it brings spiritual depression and a sense of guilt and remorse.

Unconfessed sin will drag you down. It will drain us of our peace and joy, hinder our communion with God, and give Satan an opportunity to keep us living in defeat.

He will use it as an opportunity to lead us furt' rebellion against God, where we have hardene' and refuse to hear God's voice.

We must be quick to acknowledge when we have sinned against God, to confess our sin and allow Him to cleanse and heal the wounds in our spirits.

If we allow unconfessed sin to remain, like a cancerous growth, it will spread and continue to lead us even deeper into sin and destruction.

SOMETIMES OUR SPIRITS ARE ALMOST OVERWHELMED BY OUR ENEMIES!

Sometimes, it seems like our spirits will be overwhelmed by the wounds we have received from our enemies.

The mighty warrior, David, was sorely wounded by his enemies.

His spirit was overwhelmed within him. In deep anguish he cried out to God:

> *For the enemy hath persecuted my soul; he hath smitten my life down to the ground; he hath made me to dwell in darkness, as those that have been long dead. Therefore is my spirit overwhelmed within me; my heart within me is desolate...Hear me speedily, O LORD: my spirit faileth: hide not thy face from me, lest I be like unto them that go down into the pit.*
>
> Psalm 143:3-4, 7

In our lives, many times we feel like David.

It seems the persecution from our enemies is so intense nd so persistent that our spirits feel overwhelmed; we are at e point of losing hope and are filled with despair.

It seems we have used up every ounce of human strength we have.

Our spirits are wounded and we need to be renewed, spiritually refreshed, and receive a supernatural impartation of God's dunamis power within our spirits.

You may be at the point in your life when you have experienced such an assault from your enemies, that you feel overwhelmed within your spirit.

You may be so spiritually weary that you feel you cannot go another step.

If you are at this point, God's promise to you today is:

> *For I will restore health unto thee, and I will heal thee of thy wounds, saith the LORD...*
>
> Jeremiah 30:17

Lay this book down for a minute. Stretch your hands out to God and cry out to Him, right now, as David did.

Ask Him to heal any wounds you have received from the hands of your enemies, and to restore your spiritual strength.

As you wait in His presence, He will pour the oil and the wine into your wounds and strengthen you by His Spirit within you.

You will be revived and refreshed until your spiritual strength overflows, and you are once again able to face and defeat your enemies.

HOW YOU RESPOND TO YOUR HURTS DETERMINES WHETHER YOU WILL LIVE IN VICTORY OR DEFEAT!

HOW YOU REACT AND RESPOND to the deep hurts in your life will determine whether you will live in power and victory or in weakness and defeat.

Seven strategies Satan will use to try to cause you to react to the hurts in your life which will block the healing of your wounds and keep you in a weakened condition are:

- Anger
- Withdrawal
- Self-pity
- Revenge
- Bitterness
- Unforgiveness
- Resentment

All these attitudes will cause deep wounds in your spirit, which will fester and spread unless they are healed.

If these attitudes are not dealt with, the wounds will remain long after the time you were first hurt.

Some people carry deep hurts they have received throughout their lifetime to their grave.

They put them in the back of their minds, and try to forget them.

They try to cover them up.

But, Satan will gouge and stir up those deep hurts from time to time in order to keep the individual in a weakened position.

When you are hurt or mistreated, Satan's first strategy is to try to cause you to react and respond in ANGER to the individual, or individuals, who have hurt you.

Two Greek words in the New Testament refer to anger:

The word, "ogre", is used to describe "anger", which indicates an abiding attitude of the heart, with a desire for revenge.

The word, "thumos", refers to "wrath," which describes "heated anger"..."an agitated condition of the feelings, or an outburst of the wrath from inward indignation." When we are hurt deeply by someone, especially when there seems to be no apparent reason for their actions, the reaction of our natural being is to become angry with them.

Feelings of anger begin to churn within us.

And if we yield to the anger and do not recognize it for what it is, what is in our hearts will come out of our mouths.

> ...*for out of the abundance of the heart the mouth speaketh.*
>
> Matthew 12:34

We will lash out with angry, bitter words at the individual who has hurt us, hurting them in the process.

How many times after you have you been hurt have you said harsh words which you later wished you had never spoken? How many times in a moment of anger have you acted hastily toward someone who has hurt you and were later sorry and filled with remorse? When we react or lash out in anger, we are looking for revenge...to get even, or to hurt the individual who has hurt us.

When we allow ourselves to harbor anger toward someone in our spirits, it often will result in an outburst of wrath or even blind rage.

ANGER WEAKENS OUR SPIRITS AND GIVES SATAN A FOOTHOLD!

When we have been mistreated or hurt, we must stay on guard so that we do not allow anger to remain in our hearts toward others or toward God.

Paul admonished the Ephesians

> *When angry, do not sin; do not ever let your wrath (your exasperation, your fury or indignation) last until the sun goes down. Leave no (such) room or foothold for the devil (Give no opportunity to him).*
> Ephesians 4:26-27 AMP

When we become angry without a cause to show our authority or to seek to hurt another person, it is in sin.

And, if we allow it to remain in our spirits, we are opening the door for Satan to gain a foothold in our lives, which he will use to weaken us spiritually and to destroy us.

Anger will turn into bitterness.

We must be careful not to allow any anger to remain in our spirits to brood, even overnight.

When we become angry, we must immediately get rid of it.

As long as we hold anger within our spirits, we are in grave danger.

We are actually giving Satan an opportunity to gain a stronghold in our lives.

Instead of reacting in the flesh and giving vent to our anger, we are commanded to get rid of it.

Paul said:

> *Let all bitterness and indignation and wrath (passion, rage, bad temper) and resentment (anger, animosity) and quarreling (brawling, clamor, contention) and slander (evil speaking, abusive or blasphemous language) be banished from you, with all malice (spite, ill will or baseness of any kind).*
>
> Ephesians 4:31 AMP

Paul didn't say we are to make excuses or to justify our anger, bad temper, or quarreling.

He said to get rid of it! ALL of these things...every kind or any trace...are to be completely forsaken.

If we allow anger to remain in our spirits toward another member of the Body of Christ, it not only breaks our relationship with them, it hinders our communion and fellowship with God.

Jesus warned His disciples:

> *You have heard it said to the men of old, You shall not kill; and whoever kills shall be liable to and unable to escape the punishment imposed by the court. But I say to you that every one who continues to be angry with his brother or harbors malice (enmity of heart) against him shall be liable to and unable to escape the punishment imposed by the court; and whoever speaks contemptuously*

and insultingly to his brother shall be liable to and unable to escape the punishment imposed by the Sanhedrin, and whoever says, You cursed fool! (You empty headed idiot)! Shall be viable to and unable to escape the hell (Gehenna) of fire. So if, when you are offering your gift at the altar you there remember that your brother has any (grievance) against you, Leave your gift at the altar and go. First make peace with your brother, and then come back and present your gift.

Matthew 5:21-24 AMP

In these verses, Jesus explained the danger and consequences of having anger in our spirits toward a brother.

He compared harboring anger and malice in our spirits to murder.

Murder begins with anger within the heart.

For out of the heart proceed evil thoughts, murders, adulteries, fornications, thefts, false witness, blasphemies:

Matthew 15:19

When we allow anger to remain within us, it will eventually erupt in bitter, harsh words that are spoken to hurt and destroy others.

Words spoken to other members of the Body in anger and malice from within cause deep wounds, which are capable of destroying relationships and damaging the lives of our brothers and sisters in the Lord. For this reason, when we become angry at someone who has hurt us, we must get rid of all anger, wrath, or ill will, and go to them and be reconciled.

We must be willing to forgive them and forget the wrong they have done to us.

We are not to wait for them to come to us, but we are to go to them, humble ourselves, confess, ask their forgiveness, and be reconciled to them.

Jesus said if another member of the Body of Christ has something in his heart against you, you are to leave your gift at the altar, and first go and be reconciled to them before you enter into God's Presence and offer your gifts of worship and praise (Matthew 5:23-24).

How can we expect God to accept our sacrifices of worship or the works that we do in His service while there is still anger, wrath, or malice in our hearts toward another member of the Body? We must first make every effort to be reconciled to our brother or sister in the Lord.

We must forgive all those who have mistreated us. And for those whom we may have hurt, we must seek forgiveness and make restitution wherever possible.

Confess it to God and get rid of it! Don't continue to hold onto it.

Ask God to cleanse you, and by His Spirit that is working within you, take authority over it.

Get rid of all anger you may have in your heart over past hurts and BE ON GUARD so that if you are hurt or mistreated, you do not respond in anger or allow anger to remain in your spirit.

Receive God's healing for your deep hurts and walk in a new strength!

CHOOSE TO BE A VICTOR...NOT A VICTIM!

Regardless of the deep hurts you may have experienced or will experience in the future, you never have to be defeated or destroyed.

God has given us the divine capability, through the power of the Holy Spirit, to face every trial, carry any burden, overcome every obstacle, and face every challenge in His power and strength! God has not planned any defeats for you and although you may be deeply hurt, you have a choice...either become a victim, or a victor.

As long as you allow anger, self-pity, bitterness, and unforgiveness to remain in your spirit, you will remain a victim.

Joseph endured trial after trial and faced almost every kind of injustice a person could face.

He was hated by his brothers, rejected, sold into slavery, falsely accused, misjudged, and unfairly treated, but he did not accept the role of a victim.

Instead, he told his brothers, *"You intended to harm me, but God intended it for good"* (Genesis 50:20 NIV).

Joseph knew that regardless of what his brothers or anyone else had done to destroy him, God used it to accomplish His purposes and turned it around for good.

CHAPTER THREE

One of the keys which enabled Joseph to be victorious over the hurts and trials he faced, was that he KNEW that God was in control of the circumstances of his life.

He KNEW that regardless of how discouraging or hopeless his situation looked on the surface, that God was going to make him victorious.

He chose to be a victor...not a victim! Later, when Joseph was reunited with his brothers, he acknowledged that God was in control and that it was God who had brought him to Egypt.

He said:

> *Do not be grieved or angry with yourselves, because you sold me here; for God sent me here to preserve life.*
> Genesis 45:5 NAS

> *God sent me before you to preserve for you a remnant in the earth, and to keep you alive by a great deliverance.*
> Genesis 45:7 NAS

> *Now, therefore, it was not you who sent me here, but God;*
> Genesis 45:8 NAS

Regardless of the great trials and hurts he had encountered, Joseph TRUSTED God with his whole heart.

He did not whine or complain because of the hardship and suffering he had experienced, or become disheartened, thinking God had forsaken him.

He did not place blame upon his brothers or anyone else.

He knew God was in control of the circumstances of his life and regardless of what he faced, he trusted that God would make him victorious.

It doesn't matter how difficult or trying the circumstances you may have gone through or how deep the hurts you have received in your life, you will be able to walk in victory when you know that God is in control of your circumstances and your trust is in Him.

Regardless of what others may try to do to hurt you, God will turn it around for your good. You will be able to overcome and rise above the deep hurts in your life.

In the circumstances you are facing right now, can you say that you know God is in control and that your trust is in Him to make you victorious? Don't allow past hurts, disappointments, and adverse circumstances to cloud your eyes and hinder you from believing and trusting God to accomplish the vision and purpose He has given you.

God is in control of your circumstances!

He is unlimited! Believe that what He is going to accomplish in your life is LIMITLESS! Don't be bound to what has happened to you in the past; that limits what God can and will do in your life.

Take the limits off God and trust Him! If you have ever been mistreated by a family member...falsely accused, misjudged, and unfairly treated by an employer...or have been abandoned by a friend...you will be able to identify with the deep hurts in Joseph's life.

As we look at the hurts he experienced and how he responded to those who hurt him, you will learn how to become a victor instead of a victim.

A ROOT OF BITTERNESS IN JOSEPH'S BROTHERS LED TO A MURDER PLOT!

Open your Bible to Genesis, chapter 37, and read verse 14. Joseph was only a young, seventeen-year-old man when he faced circumstances which were meant to destroy him.

He was the youngest of Jacob's sons and was his father's favorite because he had been born to him in his old age.

Although he was the youngest, Jacob favored Joseph above his older brothers.

Jacob gave Joseph the distinction of having preeminence over his brothers and expressed it by giving him a multi-colored tunic.

This tunic, or robe, was not a garment adapted for work, but was to distinguish him as being a superior or an overseer.

It had long sleeves and extended to his ankles.

Joseph's brothers saw that their father favored and loved Joseph more than them, and they hated him.

> *When his brothers saw that their father loved him more than any of them, they hated him and could not speak to him.*
>
> Genesis 37:4 NIV

They allowed a ROOT OF BITTERNESS to spring up within their spirits.

They resented and despised Joseph so much that they spoke to him with hatred and contempt.

Later, when Joseph dreamed his mother, and father, and eleven brothers bowed down before him, his brothers became jealous (Genesis 37:5-10).

The ROOT OF BITTERNESS in their life produced JEALOUSY and eventually erupted into a fit of RAGE when they planned to kill him.

Read verses 12-23.

Jacob sent Joseph to check on his brothers who were grazing the flocks near Shechem.

Joseph discovered his brothers had moved from Shechem to Dothan and he went to find them.

When his brothers saw him, they began to plot how they would kill him.

> But they saw him in the distance, and before he reached them, they plotted to kill him.
>
> Genesis 37:18 NIV

I believe that when they saw him in his multi-colored robe, the hatred, bitterness, and resentment within their spirits rose up within them and took control of them.

> Here comes the dreamer!' they said to each other. "Come now, let's kill him and throw him into one of these cisterns and say that a ferocious animal devoured him. Then we'll see what comes of his dreams.
>
> Genesis 37:19-20 NIV

47

In a fit of rage, Joseph's brothers seized him, stripped him of his robe, and threw him into a cistern.

Then, while their own brother was still down in the pit, they sat down and ate their meal.

When they saw a caravan of Ishmaelites approaching, they decided to get rid of Joseph by selling him as a slave instead of killing him.

> *So when the Midianite merchants came by, his brothers pulled Joseph up out of the cistern and sold him for twenty shekels of silver to the Ishmaelites, who took him to Egypt.*
>
> Genesis 37:28 NIV

The average price for a slave of full physical maturity was thirty shekels.

Joseph's brothers sold him into slavery for twenty pieces of silver...less than the average price for a slave!

DON'T GET CAUGHT THROWING YOURSELF A PITY PARTY!

Another major situation Satan will try to use to cause you to react to the hurts in your life, which will block the healing of your wounds and keep you in a weakened spiritual condition, is self-pity.

When we are mistreated or hurt, one of our first reactions is to become filled with self-pity.

We accept the role of a victim and begin to feel sorry for ourselves, and want others to feel sorry for us, too.

When we do what is right and are punished for it, we often cry out, "God it's not fair!" Many times when people suffer an injustice, are misjudged, slandered, or falsely accused, they wonder why God allowed them to be hurt and they begin to wallow in self-pity.

As long as they feel sorry for themselves and the way they have been mistreated, they remain victims and are bound to the hurts of their past.

When you are being hurt, never give in to self-pity or become involved in "pity parties" where you sit around feeling sorry for yourself...licking your wounds.

Self-pity will open you up to depression that will eventually lead to BITTERNESS.

Neither should you defend yourself or your actions.

When you are slandered or falsely accused, you need to communicate to correct any misunderstanding.

But you will never move out of the role of being a victim until you stop living on the defensive.

You do not need to defend yourself! You have already been justified by the work of Jesus Christ on the cross.

You have been *"justified freely by His grace through the redemption that is in Christ Jesus"* (Romans 3:24).

Regardless of what false accusations are hurled at you, you do not need to defend yourself because God is your defense.

Healing the hurts which you have received through slander and false accusations, will come as you get rid of self-pity and rely upon God to be your defense.

Self-pity will spiritually paralyze you!

As long as you continue to feel sorry for yourself...for how terribly you were mistreated...for the grave injustice done to you...for the pain and loss you have experienced... for the adverse circumstances that have come into your life such as sickness, divorce, financial problems, loss of a job or income...you will be unable to be healed of the deep hurt you have experienced.

If there are past hurts in your life where you are still feeling self-pity, GET RID OF IT NOW! Confess it to God! Tell him, "Father, I've been carrying self-pity in my spirit concerning this past hurt in my life and I want to get rid of it.

Forgive me.

I will not carry it any longer.

I release it.

Now, in the Name of Jesus, I claim healing and "new strength." Guard your spirit against self-pity.

Recognize it the moment it begins to take hold.

You may feel justified in feeling sorry for yourself because of the hurt and pain you are experiencing, or because of the way you have been mistreated. Refuse to give in to it!

Don't accept the role of a victim...CHOOSE TO BE A VICTOR!

DON'T LET YOURSELF GET BITTER!

Joseph was treated ruthlessly by his brothers.

He begged and pleaded with them for his life, but his cries fell on deaf ears as they sold him as a slave and handed him over to the Midianites and Ishmaelites (Genesis 42:21).

God had revealed to him in a dream that his mother, father, and brothers would one day bow down to him.

From being the favored son of Jacob with the multi-colored robe of honor, he became a slave and was taken from his father and mother out of his homeland and into a foreign country.

They placed shackles on his feet and put his neck in irons and led him away.

> *He (God) called down famine on the land and destroyed all their supplies of food; and he sent a man before them—Joseph, sold as a slave. They bruised his feet with shackles, his neck was put in irons, till what he foretold came to pass, till the Word of the LORD proved him true.*
>
> Psalm 105:16-19 NIV

God was in control of Joseph's circumstances and in all the adversities he faced. God was with him and upheld him during all his trials.

From the time he was led in shackles into Egypt, until he was established as a second in command to Pharaoh and his brothers bowed down to him, God's Word was tried, tested, and proved to be true.

Throughout the thirteen years of his ordeal, Joseph endured trial after trial and almost every kind of injustice an individual can face.

He was victorious over the deep hurts in his life because he never allowed anger, self-pity, resentment, or BITTERNESS to remain in his heart.

He rejected bitterness and instead of taking revenge upon his brothers, he wept over them and forgave them.

One of the major strategies Satan is using today to destroy the spiritual progress of Christians and cause confusion, division, and contention, is A ROOT OF BITTERNESS.

Our churches are filled with Christians who have allowed a root of bitterness to take hold in their spirits and it is destroying them...eating away at them like a deadly cancerous growth spreading throughout the body, killing the healthy cells.

Joseph had every opportunity to become bitter.

He suffered deep wounds at the hands of his brothers, Potiphar's wife, and Potiphar himself.

A wounded spirit is fertile ground for a ROOT OF BITTERNESS to take hold.

When spirits are deeply wounded, bitterness will immediately try to take root, if we allow it.

Joseph was taken in chains to Egypt, where he was sold to a nobleman named Potiphar...

Now Joseph had been taken down to Egypt. Potiphar, an Egyptian who was one of Pharaoh's officials, the captain of the guard, bought him from the Ishmaelites who had taken him there.

Genesis 39:1 NIV

In these circumstances Joseph did not become bitter toward his brothers or toward God.

Many times when Christians have been deeply hurt by the mistreatment or adverse circumstances they experience in life, they not only hold bitterness in their spirit toward those who have hurt them, but they blame God for allowing the pain and adversity to come into their lives.

If they allow the root of bitterness to remain, it continues to grow. And as it grows it causes SPIRITUAL BLINDNESS where they cannot see their true spiritual condition.

The root of bitterness in their lives distorts their judgment and blocks them from the healing of their wounds.

THE ROOT OF BITTERNESS IS A DEADLY POISON THAT WILL TORMENT AND DESTROY YOU!

A major key in being victorious over a root of bitterness is recognizing it the moment it begins to try to take hold in your spirit and then rejecting it.

The thing that will cause the hurts you experience in your life to develop into a root of bitterness, is your failure to respond to the help that God can give you at the time of being hurt.

When you become grievously wounded...regardless of how deeply you may feel the pain...regardless of who has hurt you...instead of nursing your wounds or allowing feelings of anger and self-pity to overwhelm you, you must immediately go to the Lord and pour out your heart to Him.

Some people make the mistake of going to a close friend to share their pain, which often only adds fuel to the fire and feeds the spirits that you need to get rid of.

Jesus came to heal the brokenhearted and bind up the wounds of those who are bruised and broken.

There are times when it is good to have someone to console and support you when you have been deeply hurt, but He alone can heal the wounds of a broken spirit.

The root of bitterness is like a plant.

When it takes root, it goes deep down into the spirit.

After a person has become wounded, the root of bitterness may not appear on the surface.

The person may not even realize they have a root of bitterness in their spirit.

But, if it is allowed to remain, it will eventually grow and produce bitter fruit.

Out of the innermost being will emerge bitter, harsh words and bitter actions toward the person who has hurt them, and as long as the person harbors bitterness and resentment in their spirit toward someone else, it cuts off the relationship with that person and with God.

Bitterness will poison our spirits and defile our relationship with others.

Paul warned the Hebrews to SET A WATCH and guard themselves from allowing a root of bitterness to spring up between them.

He told them:

> *Exercise foresight and be on watch to look (after one another), to see that no one falls back from and fails to secure God's grace (His unmerited favor and spiritual blessing), in order that no root of resentment (rancor, BITTERNESS or hatred) shoots forth and causes trouble and bitter torment, and the many become contaminated and defiled by it.*
>
> Hebrews 12:15 AMP

Bitterness causes torment.

It not only will destroy the Christian who has the root of bitterness in his spirit, but Paul said it will DEFILE AND CONTAMINATE MANY OTHERS.

We must SET A WATCH, refusing to allow a root of bitterness to spring forth.

Today, we must not only SET A WATCH and GUARD our spirits from becoming contaminated by a root of bitterness, we must pluck up by the roots any bitterness we may have in our spirits over hurts we have received in the past.

A root of bitterness bears bitter fruit.

You cannot hide it.

Like a weed, you can cut off the top portion of the weed and level it to the ground. But, as long as the root remains it will continue to grow and crop up time and time again.

In due time, the fruit of bitterness will appear.

The effects of bitterness are not localized.

The root of bitterness in one person can poison an entire family, an entire business organization, an entire church congregation, or an entire community.

Its deadly poison spreads, defiles people, and makes them unfit to stand before God.

It not only affects them, but also has wide-ranging effects...it defiles MANY! The root of bitterness leads to REBELLION, which is the sin of witchcraft.

These sins, which God has revealed to me, are so prevalent in churches today.

Satan is using bitterness and rebellion to destroy the lives of Christians, SOW SEEDS OF DISCONTENT AND DISCORD, and bring CONTENTION and DIVISION within the Body of Christ.

Next month we will go more in-depth into the root of bitterness, its deadly poison and effects upon those who allow it to remain in their spirits, as well as how to get rid of it.

RESENTMENT WILL KEEP YOU WOUNDED!

Although he was falsely accused, lied about by Potiphar's wife, and mistreated and misjudged by Potiphar, Joseph did not allow resentment to take hold in his spirit.

He knew that regardless of the mistreatment or hurts that he had received at the hands of these people, God was with him. This enabled him to be victorious even in what seemed to be the most discouraging circumstances.

Joseph did not allow his hurts to defeat him, but kept his eyes on God.

Even as a slave in Potiphar's house, Joseph prospered and was blessed.

> *The LORD was with Joseph and he prospered, and he lived in the house of his Egyptian master. When his master saw that the LORD was with him and that the LORD gave him success in everything he did, Joseph found favor in his eyes and became his attendant. Potiphar put him in charge of his household, and he entrusted to his care everything he owned. From the time he put him in charge of his household and of all that he owned, the LORD blessed the household of the Egyptian because of Joseph. The blessing of the LORD was on everything Potiphar had, both in the house and in the field.*
>
> Genesis 39:2-5 NIV

Joseph may have been a slave in the land of Egypt, but he was not a victim! He did not harbor resentment in his spirit toward Potiphar, nor toward his brothers, nor towards God for what happened to him.

His brothers had intended to destroy him.

They thought he would live the rest of his life as a slave in the land of Egypt...that his life would be filled with pain, trials, and hard labor.

But God took Joseph's hurts and his circumstances, and turned them around for his good.

Even after Potiphar's wife tried to seduce Joseph and falsely accused him of attacking her, and Potiphar threw him into prison, God was with him.

He may have been a prisoner far away from his home in the land of Egypt, but he was not a victim! God caused him to prosper even while he was in prison and gave him favor in the eyes of the prison warden.

> ...*But while Joseph was there in the prison, the* LORD *was with him; he showed him kindness and granted him favor in the eyes of the prison warden. So the warden put Joseph in charge of all those held in the prison, and he was made responsible for all that was done there. The warden paid no attention to anything under Joseph's care, because the* LORD *was with Joseph and gave him success in whatever he did.*
>
> Genesis 39:20-23 NIV

God had not forsaken Joseph.

He saw his sufferings and IN THE MIDST of his hurts and circumstance, He caused him to prosper in everything he did.

All these things God allowed in Joseph's life were being used by God to test and prepare him for what God had planned for his life as governor over Egypt.

While he was in prison he did not become resentful towards Potiphar's wife for slandering him.

Even though he was unjustly accused and thrown into prison, he did not allow himself to burn with hatred toward Potiphar, whom he served loyally and faithfully.

RESENTMENT WILL KEEP YOU SPIRITUALLY CRIPPLED!

You may have been hurt and you felt as if you were at the very bottom of the barrel with no way out.

Even now you may feel what Joseph must have felt when he was first thrown into prison: weary, discouraged, ready to give up.

You may have been mistreated by someone you loved and you are heartbroken.

Whatever you do, do not allow resentment toward the person who has hurt you to fill your spirit.

It will hinder the healing oil of God from flowing into your life, and it will destroy you!

RECEIVE GOD'S HEALING FOR YOUR DEEP HURTS!

In this end-time hour, God wants to bring the Body of Christ to a new position of TOTAL WHOLENESS-spirit, soul, and body.

By His Spirit, He is calling us to bring to Him all the hurts and broken areas in our lives where we need healing and deliverance.

His promise to us today is:

> *For I will restore health unto thee, and I will heal thee of thy wounds, saith the LORD...*
> Jeremiah 30:17

Concerning God's purpose for the Church, Paul said:

> *His intention was the perfecting and the full equipping of*

the saints (His consecrated people), (that they should do) the work of ministering toward building up Christ's Body (the Church), (that it might develop) until we all attain oneness in the faith and in the comprehension of the full and accurate knowledge of the Son of God; that (we might arrive) at really mature manhood — the completeness of personality which is nothing less that the standard height of Christ's own perfection, the measure of the stature of the fullness of the Christ and the completeness found in Him.

Ephesians 4:12-13 AMP

God's plan for our lives is that He is going to PERFECT and bring us into a place of COMPLETION, where we have grown into full maturity...to the full stature of Jesus Christ, where we have attained the fullness of Christ.

Jesus prayed for the Church that we would be PERFECTED.

He said:

I in them, and thou in me, that they may be made perfect in one.

John 17:23

Circle the word "perfect" in this verse.

It is translated from the Greek word "teleiosis," which means "to bring to an end by completing or perfecting," and in this verse refers to the bringing to completeness of His saints.

In this end-time harvest, God is going to bring us to a place of COMPLETENESS...of TOTAL WHOLENESS...where we have grown up and fully matured in all aspects into Christ...where His life is fully manifested in us.

In this position of TOTAL WHOLENESS, nothing in our lives will be lacking.

We will be COMPLETE in Christ, possessing His fullness! Praise the Name of God! Before we teach this position of full maturity, God is going to bring healing and restoration to the Body of Christ.

He wants us to experience healing in every area of our lives.

He wants to bind up the wounds and strengthen the areas where we are weak.

He wants to cleanse and purge us of those things that hinder our spiritual growth.

We will not be able to reach this position of completeness...TOTAL WHOLENESS...so long as we are still carrying wounds from our past...living in defeat...holding onto bitterness, resentment, and unforgiveness.

It is time for us to get rid of the things in our lives that are causing us to live in a weakened spiritual condition.

Allow the Spirit of God to speak to you.

Open up your spirit to God and allow Him to remove any anger, bitterness, self-pity, resentment, and unforgiveness.

Let Him pour the oil and wine into the deep wounds in your life, and strengthen and restore you to a place of TOTAL WHOLENESS.

WITHDRAWAL ISN'T THE ANSWER!

When an individual has been hurt deeply many times, they will often withdraw and cease to communicate so they will never get hurt again.

They put up barriers so that no one can get close to them.

They refuse to open up and trust others.

They say they have forgiven the one who has hurt them, yet they refuse to have fellowship with that person.

Instead of restoring the relationship, they keep the other person at a distance. Most are afraid to love again and harden their hearts toward the individual that hurt them.

When we cut ourselves off from other members of the Body, we are actually hurting ourselves and weakening the Body of Christ.

God has placed members within the Body, placing us together in such a way that we are all dependent upon one another.

We are all members of the same Body. We cannot say to the other members that we do not need them.

Paul said:

> *And the eye cannot say to the hand, "I have no need of you;" or again the head to the feet, "I have no need of you" ...But God has so composed the body, giving more abundant honor to that member which lacked, so that there may be no division in the body, but that the members may have the same care for one another. And if one member suffers, all the members suffer with it; if one member is honored, all the members rejoice with it.*
>
> I Corinthians 12:21, 24-26 NAS

As long as members have cut themselves off from other members and there are broken relationships, there is division in the Body of Christ.

God wants to pour the oil of the Holy Spirit into those wounds to soften the hearts of those who have hardened their hearts toward other members of the Body.

He wants to set them free to have communion with other members so they will be strengthened and made whole.

When others hurt us deeply, instead of cutting ourselves off and building barriers, we must be tenderhearted and forgiving and restore the fellowship.

Instead of holding onto the hurt, we must RELEASE it by releasing God's love toward the individual who has hurt us.

Paul said,

> *Let all bitterness, and wrath, and anger, and clamor, and evil speaking, be put away from you, with all malice: And be ye kind one to another, tenderhearted,*

forgiving one another, even as God for Christ's sake hath forgiven you.

Ephesians 4:31, 32

When you have been deeply hurt, loving the person who has hurt you is probably the farthest thing from your mind.

Feelings of anger and bitterness will rise up within you.

Releasing God's love will require an act of your will.

Don't wait until you feel like it! As an act of your will, choose to love the person with God's love.

God's love is not resentful and does not take into account the wrong or evil which has been done, but it is strong and enduring.

Concerning God's love, Paul said:, *"Love bears up under anything and everything that comes, is ever ready to believe the best of every person, its hopes are fadeless under all circumstances and it endures everything (without weakening)."*

I Corinthians 13:7 AMP

You may be carrying deep hurts from your past which have caused you to cut yourself off from your feelings, or cut yourself off from relationships with family members...a husband or wife, child, parent...a close friend...another member of the Body...a fellow employee.

Don't continue to hold on to that hurt.

Release that hurt now and allow God to heal you.

You do not have to remain a victim...CHOOSE to be a victor! Release God's love toward those who have hurt you.

CHOOSE to love them with God's love! God will rebuild and restore relationships.

He will soften your heart and set you free to open yourself up to love and enjoy fellowship with others.

DON'T TAKE REVENGE!

Throughout the thirteen years of Joseph's slavery and imprisonment, he had plenty of time to plot his revenge against his brothers.

But he didn't.

He had plenty of time to allow himself to become bitter toward his brothers, to cut himself off from any further relationship with them.

But he didn't.

Joseph refused to be a victim.

He refused to be consumed by bitterness.

Instead, he continued to love his brothers despite what they had done, and looked forward to the day when he would see them and his father again.

God did not leave Joseph alone while he was in prison either.

His brothers may have forgotten him...but God was with him, directing events to deliver Joseph out of prison and fulfill His plan for Joseph's life.

While he was in prison, Pharaoh's cupbearer and baker were confined to prison and placed in Joseph's charge.

During their time of confinement, both of the men had dreams that Joseph interpreted.

Upon their release, both of the dreams came true, just as Joseph had interpreted.

However, the cupbearer forgot about Joseph and it was not until two years later that he remembered him.

When Pharaoh had a dream, he called for the wise men and magicians to interpret the dream.

None of them could interpret it.

The cupbearer remembered that while he was in prison, Joseph had correctly interpreted his dream and he told Pharaoh this.

Pharaoh sent for Joseph, who interpreted his dream.

In all of these circumstances, God was in control, directing and working on Joseph's behalf to fulfill His plan for Joseph's life.

Pharaoh rewarded Joseph by placing him in charge of his palace, and putting him second in command over Egypt.

> *Then Pharaoh said to Joseph, "Since God has made all this known to you, there is no one so discerning and wise as you. You shall be in charge of my palace, and all my people are to submit to your orders. Only with respect to the throne will I be greater than you. So Pharaoh said to Joseph, "I hereby put you in charge of*

the whole land of Egypt.

Genesis 41:39-41 NIV

Joseph was hated, rejected, and sold into slavery by his own brothers. He was falsely accused and slandered by Potiphar's wife. He was misjudged by Potiphar and thrown into prison, but he was victorious over all these things because he never accepted the role of a victim! He kept his faith and trust in God.

He later told his brothers, *"You intended to harm me, but God intended it for good..."* (Genesis 50:20 NIV).

In all these things, Joseph saw the hand of God overruling the plans of his brothers.

Instead of seeking revenge, he looked for healing and the restoration of his relationship with his brothers.

Instead of anger and bitterness, he forgave them and wept over them. He did not wait until they asked for his forgiveness; he forgave them willingly and eagerly.

After Joseph's brothers returned a second time with Benjamin and appeared before him, Joseph could not restrain himself any longer, and amid his tears, revealed himself to his brothers.

Then Joseph could no longer control himself before all his attendants, and he cried out, "Have everyone leave my presence!" So there was no one with Joseph when he made himself known to his brothers.

And he wept so loudly that the Egyptians heard him, and Pharaoh's household heard about it.

Genesis 45:2 NIV

Joseph called his brothers close to him and said,

> *...I am your brother Joseph, the one you sold into Egypt!*
>
> Genesis 45:4 NIV

In all his dealings with his brothers, there was not even the slightest trace of vindictiveness.

Not once did he reproach them for selling him into slavery.

Not once did he remind them his heart had been broken and crushed because of their hatred and bitterness toward him.

Instead, he ministered to them and told them not to be distressed or angry with themselves for how they had mistreated him.

Weeping, he threw his arms around Benjamin and kissed his brothers, not with self-pity for how he had been mistreated or because of his deep hurt, but because he had been restored to his brothers.

INSTEAD OF REVENGE, WE MUST SEEK RESTORATION AND RECONCILIATION!

This is a powerful example of how we must react to the deep hurts in our lives, especially in our relationships with other members of the Body of Christ.

When we are misjudged, misunderstood, mistreated, or deeply hurt by others within the Body of Christ, our major concern must be RESTORATION and RECONCILIATION, instead of revenge.

Many times, when people are hurt they inwardly look forward to the time when they will be able to "get even" with the person who mistreated them.

They rejoice when the person who has hurt them experiences pain or trouble, thinking, "It serves them right for how they mistreated me." Our response toward the mistreatment and hurts we receive ought to be like Joseph's.

When we are hurt, we must freely forgive and eagerly work toward the day of restoration and reconciliation of our relationship with our brother or sister in the Lord.

We must never seek revenge, only healing and restoration.

Paul told the Romans:

> *Do not repay anyone evil for evil. Be careful to do what is right in the eyes of everybody. If it is possible, as far as it depends on you, live at peace with everyone. Do not take revenge, my friends, but leave room for God's wrath, for it is written: "It is mine to avenge; I will repay," says the Lord. On the contrary: "If your enemy is hungry, feed him; if he is thirsty, give him something to drink. In doing this, you will heap burning coals on his head." Do not be overcome by evil, but overcome evil with good.*
>
> Romans 12:17-21 NIV

When we have been mistreated or hurt, we have a choice...to be a victim and be overcome, or to be a victor and overcome.

Paul said, "Don't let yourself be overcome by evil." Don't allow the evil things people may do against you to overcome you.

Be a victor! Overcome the evil things that are said or done against you by doing good to those who hurt you.

FORGIVE!

One of the major strategies Satan is using today to bring division within the Church and keep Christians living in a weakened spiritual condition, is UNFORGIVENESS.

When we allow unforgiveness to remain in our spirits against someone who has hurt us, it blocks the healing of our wounds and it hinders our relationship with God and will keep us in defeat.

Knowing that we are required by God to forgive, and that forgiveness by God depends upon our willingness to forgive others, we forgive those who have hurt us with this attitude, "I know that I must forgive you, but I cannot forget what you did to me." And from that point on we keep the person at a distance and still hold a grudge against them.

Joseph fully and completely forgave his brothers for the grave injustice and mistreatment he had suffered at their hands.

He drew them close to himself, embraced them, and wept over them.

His forgiveness was not just an emotional reaction or a temporary thing.

It was heartfelt and genuine.

After their father died, Joseph's brothers became worried that Joseph would then take revenge upon them.

They said amongst themselves,

What if Joseph holds a grudge against us and pays us back for all the wrong we did to him?

Genesis 50:15 NIV

They sent a message to Joseph saying,

..."Your father left these instructions before he died: 'This is what you are to say to Joseph: I ask you to forgive your brothers the sins and the wrongs they committed in treating you so badly.' Now please forgive the sins of the servants of the God of your father." *(When their message came to him, Joseph wept).*

Genesis 50:16-17 NIV

He loved his brothers and had already forgiven them completely for all that they had done to hurt him.

His brothers then came and threw themselves down before him. "We are your slaves," they said.

Genesis 50:18 NIV

Joseph said:

...don't be afraid.

Am I in the place of God? You intended to harm me, but God intended it for good to accomplish what is now being done, the saving of many lives.

So then, don't be afraid.

I will provide for you and your children.' And he reassured them and spoke kindly to them.

Genesis 50:19-21 NIV

Joseph harbored no bitterness or ill will whatsoever toward his brothers.

There was absolutely nothing in his heart against them.

He was a victor, not a victim.

He had forgiven them and RELEASED the past with its hurts and was healed and set free.

When we hurt, our responsibility before God is to forgive and RELEASE the past, no matter how deeply we may have been hurt, or what the other person does.

It doesn't matter whether or not we feel like forgiving.

We may have been hurt so badly that we may feel we are incapable of forgiving the person who has hurt us.

Even though we know we should forgive and let go of the hurts of our past, we are bound to the past by our feelings.

We feel angry, violated, and victimized.

The hurt goes on hurting.

True forgiveness is the key to being set free and of the wounds of the past being healed.

When we are hurt, we have a choice...to hold onto our unforgiveness and remain a victim, or to choose to forgive and become whole once again.

WE MUST FORGIVE WITH THE SAME UNLIMITED FORGIVENESS CHRIST HAS GIVEN US!

Our concept of forgiveness has been too limited! We are willing to forgive as long as the person who has mistreated us will apologize.

Often we put limitations on forgiveness.

We forgive those who hurt us, but often we are watching every step they make as if they are on probation.

True forgiveness doesn't depend on the reactions of anyone else.

True forgiveness is complete.

True forgiveness erases blame.

True forgiveness is continual.

The type of forgiveness we are to have toward others is to be ACCORDING TO THE FORGIVENESS WE HAVE RECEIVED FROM CHRIST! Paul said:

> *Put on therefore, as the elect of God, holy and beloved, bowels of mercies, kindness, humbleness of mind, meekness, long suffering; Forbearing one another, and forgiving one another, if any man have a quarrel against any: even as Christ forgave you, so also do ye.*
>
> Colossians 3:12-13

"EVEN AS CHRIST FORGAVE YOU, SO ALSO DO YE." This is not something that is optional, according to whether or not we feel like forgiving others.

It is required of us and if we fail to do so, we are giving Satan an opportunity to keep us in a weakened spiritual condition.

Jesus endured intense suffering and mistreatment.

He was wounded in the house of His friends (Zechariah 13:6).

He was misunderstood, misjudged, falsely accused, and betrayed by His closest and dearest friends.

He was reviled, blasphemed, mocked, ridiculed, beaten, tortured, and killed.

How did he respond to the intense suffering and wounds. He received from those He came to save? He never demonstrated any response other than forgiveness and unconditional love!

> *He was guilty of no sin, neither was deceit (guile) ever found on His lips. When He was reviled and insulted, He did not revile or offer insult in return; He made no threats (of vengeance); but He trusted (Himself and everything) to Him Who judges fairly.*
> I Peter 2:22-23 AMP

As Jesus hung on the cross...wounded, broken, bleeding, dying...even while His accusers were mocking Him, His prayer was, *"Father, forgive them, for they know not what they do."* (Luke 23:34).

This is the SAME type of forgiveness we must have toward those who abuse, mistreat, slander, and hurt us! That means you must be willing to forgive all those who may have hurt you in the past...an unfaithful husband or wife...a rebellious child...an abusive parent...an employer who treated you unfairly...a member of the Body who misrepresented you and slandered your good name...WITH THAT SAME UNLIMITED FORGIVENESS.

CHOOSE TO BE A VICTOR...GET RID OF UNFORGIVENESS!

You may think, "I don't have the same type of forgiveness...I want to forgive, but I don't know if I can."

You may be still suffering from the pain you experienced and do not feel like forgiving the person who hurt you.

Regardless of how you may feel, you must be willing to forgive as Christ has freely forgiven you.

As an act of your will, you must CHOOSE to forgive.

If you feel you do not have forgiveness in your heart, ask Christ to let His love, grace, and forgiveness flow through you.

The person who allows unforgiveness to remain in his spirit toward those who have hurt him is not only hindering the healing of his wounds and the restoration of his relationship, but is GIVING Satan an opportunity to keep him in a weakened position.

Paul told the Corinthians:

> *To whom ye forgive any thing, I forgive also: for if I forgave any thing, to whom I forgave it, for your sakes forgave I it in the person of Christ; Lest Satan should get an advantage of us: for we are not ignorant of his devices.*
>
> II Corinthians 2:10-11

When we allow unforgiveness to remain in our spirits, we are giving Satan an advantage: an entrance to defeat us.

I believe one of the reasons many Christians are not receiving more answers to their prayers is because they are harboring unforgiveness and resentment in their hearts against others.

Jesus has made it very clear that unless we are willing to forgive one another, we cannot be forgiven.

75

When He taught His disciples how to pray, He included forgiveness as part of the prayer:

> *For if ye forgive men their trespasses, your heavenly Father will also forgive you: But if ye forgive not men their trespasses, neither will your Father forgive your trespasses.*
>
> Matthew 6:14-15

Our forgiveness and acceptance by God depends upon the forgiveness we have toward one another.

When other members of the Body of Christ make mistakes or sin against God, instead of criticizing and ostracizing them, God wants us to go to them in love and extend God's grace and forgiveness toward them.

Instead of judging and condemning them, He wants us to stand with them...to pray the problem through together and restore them in love.

When others sin against us, instead of lashing out in anger or cutting off our relationship with them, God wants us to forgive and be reconciled to them.

True forgiveness is the key that will liberate you and set you free from the hurts of your past.

If you are still holding unforgiveness in your spirit toward someone who has hurt you in the past, it is time you get rid of it! God wants to pour the oil and wine into your hurts and restore you to a new position of strength of TOTAL WHOLENESS.

Confess the unforgiveness in your heart to God.

Pour out to Him the pain and hurt that you feel.

Remember, there is no hurt too deep or grief too great that Christ cannot heal.

He knows what it means to be rejected, mistreated, and wounded.

He feels your pain and sorrow.

Regardless of how deeply you may have been hurt or may be hurting today, those hurts cannot overwhelm or destroy you.

You do not have to remain a victim, bound by the hurts of the past.

CHOOSE to be a victor!

Get rid of the unforgiveness in your heart.

Tell God, "I choose to forgive my father or mother for rejecting, abusing, or mistreating me." "I choose to forgive my husband who has been unfaithful to me." "I choose to forgive my wife who has divorced me...to forgive my rebellious teenager." Whoever has hurt you and whatever they may have done, as an act of your will, CHOOSE to forgive them.

Be specific in your prayers.

Call out their name and explain how they have hurt you.

Then ask God to allow His forgiveness to flow through you.

As you do this, God is going to set you free and heal the deep wounds in your life.

God's promise to you today is:

> *For I will restore health unto thee, and I will heal thee of thy wounds, saith the Lord...*
>
> Jeremiah 30:17

GET RID OF THE ROOT OF BITTERNESS AND REBELLION!

A time of healing and restoration is coming to the Body of Christ! God is going to pour the healing oil of the Holy Spirit into the deep wounds the Body of Christ has experienced within the past few years.

Scandals involving immorality, covetousness, selfishness, and greed within major ministries and among Christians leaders have left many Christians spiritually wounded. Members of the Body have become cynical and suspicious of one another, especially of those in leadership positions.

With the fall of prominent Christian leaders and ministers in the past few years, there has been a great sense of loss. Many Christians feel as if their faith and trust have been betrayed. As a result, there is a lack of trust and confidence toward Christian leaders, ministers, and especially television evangelists and television ministries.

Satan has been using these past wounds to keep the Body of Christ in a spiritually weakened condition...vulnerable to his attacks. As long as these deep wounds remain, we will remain in a weakened position and it will give Satan an opening for further attack. The same is true individually. As long as you may be holding onto hurts and mistakes of your past, you will remain in a weakened position and Satan will use this opening to further attack you.

CHAPTER FOUR

In the natural realm, what happens when an individual is wounded-receives a cut on his hand, foot, or any other part of his body? He immediately cleanses the wound with an antiseptic and protects it by placing a bandage over it. Why? He knows there is the possibility of the wound becoming infected. The infection could enter his bloodstream and eventually spread throughout his entire body, causing even further damage. Gangrene could set in, and the affected limb would need to be amputated, or in some cases, the bloodstream could become infected and eventually cause death.

The same is true in the spiritual realm. When a Christian's spirit becomes wounded, the wound must be cleansed and healed by the Holy Spirit. If not it will fester, becoming gangrenous and eventually spread, contaminating his entire spirit and hindering his spiritual growth.

If the wounds Christians have experienced throughout the Body of Christ – through sin, anger, self-pity, bitterness, resentment, revenge, unforgiveness – are not cleansed and healed, they will fester and spread throughout the entire Body of Christ, hindering its spiritual growth.

THE ROOT OF BITTERNESS PRODUCES BITTER FRUIT!

The root of bitterness does not always appear on the surface. It is possible for an individual to cover up bitterness and carry it with him for years without detection. Many Christians have been deeply hurt, but have tried to hide it or pretend it is not there. They do not want to recognize the fact they are vulnerable. They feel that if they admit they have been hurt, they will appear weak or that other Christians will look down on them. They try to put the hurt out of their minds or blot it out; but covering it up and refusing to acknowledge it only causes more pain and blocks further healing.

Many husbands and wives have been carrying bitterness toward one another in their spirits for years because of some past hurt. Many adults have been carrying bitterness in their spirits toward a parent concerning hurts they experienced in their childhood. These individuals have been afraid to openly acknowledge these hurts because of a fear of how the other person will react and the possibility of being further hurt.

The root of bitterness goes down very deep into the spirit. And if it is allowed to remain, it will eventually grow and produce bitter fruit. An individual who is harboring bitterness in his spirit toward someone else will eventually manifest that bitterness through his words and actions. You cannot hide it. Like a weed, you can cut off the top portion of a weed level with the ground, but as long as the root remains, it will continue to grow and crop up time and time again. In due time the fruit of bitterness will appear.

The root of bitterness that has spread throughout the Body of Christ must be PLUCKED UP BY THE ROOT! Bitterness brings TORMENT. Paul warned the believers to SET A WATCH and BE ON THE LOOKOUT so that a root of bitterness would not rise up among them "and cause trouble and bitter torment."

As long as we allow bitterness to remain in our spirits toward someone who has hurt us, Satan will bombard our minds with thoughts concerning the injustice and what the other person has done to hurt us, and will stir up our emotions until we are TORMENTED.

Just when it seems we have been able to get over our hurt and put it out of our minds, he will stir it up again, or we will experience another hurt which will bring back all the past hurts to our minds. Feelings of anger and bitterness will try to control our actions. We cannot allow our feelings and emotions to rule us, but we must learn how to take control of them and walk in the Spirit, not according to the dictates of our flesh.

Not only will bitterness bring torment, it will POISON our spirits. As bitterness takes root, it causes spiritual blindness where we are unable to see the truth clearly. It distorts our judgment. It blinds us from seeing God's healing for our hurts and hinders us from seeing our true spiritual condition,which has become contaminated by anger, bitterness, and unforgiveness. Our eyes become focused only upon the hurt, how badly the other person has treated us, or upon why God allowed us to be hurt and experience pain and tragedy.

BITTERNESS BRINGS BONDAGE!

Bitterness brings anguish and misery. That individual who has become bitter not only suffers from the pain of the hurt that he has experienced, but he is in spiritual bondage... chained to the past and bound to those who have hurt him. As long as he allows bitterness to remain in his heart toward someone who has hurt him or concerning the adverse circumstances or tragedies he has experienced, he will remain emotionally bound to that person. The bitterness binds him to the person who has hurt him, and that person will continue to control his emotions and responses.

If every time we come in contact with those who have hurt us and our minds are bombarded with all that they have done in the past to hurt us, where anger and resentment rise up within us, that is a clear indication that a root of bitterness remains. Every trace must be plucked out by the root.

BITTERNESS IN THE SPIRIT...PRODUCES A BITTER, POISONOUS TONGUE!

As the poison of bitterness spreads and takes hold within the individual's spirit, bitter, malicious words will begin to spew forth. Out of the bitter torment and anguish of his spirit will come harsh, angry words directed at those who have hurt him or toward God. The person who is bitter will become critical, and will begin to murmur and complain or use his tongue as a poisonous weapon to get revenge upon those who have hurt him.

Out of the intense pain, suffering, and bitterness of his spirit, Job cried out, *"I will not restrain my mouth; I will speak in the anguish of my spirit, I will complain in the bitterness of my soul"* (Job 7:11, NAS). Job attributed his pain and suffering to God, and the root of bitterness within him could not be restrained. He inwardly blamed God and voiced his complaint.

He said:

> *If I called, and He answered me, I could not believe that He was listening to my voice. For He bruises me with a tempest and multiplied my wounds without cause. He will not allow me to get my breath, but saturates me with bitterness.*
>
> Job 9:16-18 NAS

From the depths of Job's spirit came his bitter complaint.

> *Even today is my complaint rebellious and bitter; my stroke is heavier than my groaning. Oh, that I knew where I might find Him, that I might come even to His*

seat! I would lay my cause before Him, and fill my mouth with arguments.

Job 23:2-4 AMP

Bitterness blinded Job and destroyed his judgment. He did not see that behind the circumstances he faced...the loss of his children, the loss of his livestock, the terrible affliction of boils upon his body...Satan was responsible and was using his circumstances to destroy him and cause him to question God. He was filled with hopelessness and despair and could not see God's deliverance. He could not see his true spiritual condition, but continued to justify himself before God. It was not until he repented that God healed him and turned his captivity around.

He was ready to die. He said:

I loathe my very life; therefore I will give free rein to my complaint and speak out in the bitterness of my soul. I will say to God: Do not condemn me, but tell me what charges you have against me. Does it please you to oppress me, to spurn the work of your hands, while you smile on the schemes of the wicked?

Job 10:1-3 NIV

Today, people like Job, in their pain and suffering have become bitter toward God and are sending forth bitter complaints towards Him. They do not understand why God has allowed them to be so deeply hurt...why He has not delivered them out of their pain and suffering...why He has allowed others to mistreat them so badly. They do not recognize their bitter complaints as rebellion against God.

Christians in churches today have become bitter toward the pastor or other members of the congregation, and their tongues have become poisonous weapons used by Satan to spread bitterness, discontent, strife, and division.

The root of bitterness has taken hold within the Body of Christ and has spread its poisonous gall throughout a great majority of our churches. Christians who have become bitter toward other members of the Body of Christ, their pastor or other Christian leaders, are speaking forth bitter, harsh words...spreading gossip, tearing down, and trying to destroy the reputation of holy men and women of God.

BITTERNESS CONTAMINATES AND SPREADS LIKE A DEADLY CANCER!

It is time for us to expose this root of bitterness wherever it may be found. Not only does bitterness contaminate the spirit of the individual who has been hurt, it spreads and multiplies. Paul said:

> ...many become contaminated and defiled by it.
> Hebrews 12:15 AMP

A root of bitterness springs up within a church and spreads when a member, out of the hurt and bitterness of his spirit, begins to tear down and criticize the pastor, sows discord, and continually finds fault. The words coming forth out of his mouth are poisonous, and before long there are others who have joined with him in speaking harsh, bitter words.

No doubt you may have heard someone who has become bitter toward his pastor, church, or employer and he has so much bitterness stored up within him he never has a good word to say about anything. People like this continually talk about how badly or unjustly they were treated. Out of their bitter spirits, they hurl unjust accusations, slander, and undermine those in authority.

RISE UP IN YOUR SPIRIT AND RULE OVER YOUR FEELINGS AND EMOTIONS!

God is bringing healing and restoration to the Church whereby we will experience TOTAL WHOLENESS...SPIRIT...SOUL...BODY! Our spirits have been infused and empowered by the Sprit of God! The very life of Christ has been manifested within us! We have access to an IMMEASURABLE...INEXHAUSTIBLE supply of His strength! Through His DUNAMIS... miracle-working power that is in our spirits, we have the ability and capability to face every trial, carry any burden, overcome every obstacle, and face every challenge in the power of His MIGHT!

You don't have to be bound by hurts from your past any longer. God wants to set you free! Through His Word, He wants to reveal any past hurts or unconfessed sins, cleanse those wounds and pour in the oil and wine of the Holy Spirit, totally heal them, and make you WHOLE!

God is saying to us, "DON'T LOOK BACK...Don't hold onto those past hurts any longer!" DON'T LOOK BACK...Don't keep dragging up the past and "rehashing" old memories of how you have been hurt. It's time for us to put those things behind us and walk in a new dimension of spiritual maturity and strength.

One of the major strategies Satan is using to keep Christians in a spiritually weakened position, where they are chained to the hurts of the past, is to try to cause them to live ACCORDING TO THEIR FEELINGS, where they are controlled by their own emotions.

CHAPTER FIVE

Before healing of past hurts can take place and we can experience TOTAL WHOLENESS, healing must take place in our emotions.

We are going beyond the surface, deep into the spirit realm, to the battlefield of our SOULS...to take control over our FEELINGS and EMOTIONS and bring them into submission to the Holy Spirit.

God has planned that every aspect of man's being...spirit, soul and body...be TOTALLY WHOLE and the soul and the body be RULED by the Spirit of God within man's spirit. Our lives are to be ruled and regulated by the Spirit, not by the dictates of our flesh. When our spirits (inner man) have been infused by His MIGHT...His DUNAMIS, miracle-working power...we are able to draw upon His IMMEASURABLE, INEXHAUSTIBLE supply of strength and bring our souls and bodies into submission to the Spirit of God within us.

Paul prayed for the Ephesians:

> *May He grant you out of the rich treasury of His glory to be strengthened and reinforced with mighty power in the inner man by the [Holy] Spirit [Himself indwelling your innermost being and personality].*
> Ephesians 3:16 AMP

He said:

> *...Be strong in the Lord [be empowered through your union with him]; draw strength from Him [that strength which His boundless might provides].*
> Ephesians 6:10 AMP

We have no excuse for being spiritually weak and anemic! Through our union with Christ, whose resurrection life dwells within us, we have access to His power; but we must draw our strength from Him.

When our spirits become wounded, weakened, or broken, our souls and bodies are affected and our entire being is weakened. When our spirits are weak, our minds become filled with doubt, fear, unbelief, and every sort of negative thought. We are ruled by our feelings and emotions; and unless we draw upon God's MIGHT and rise up in the Spirit to bring our thoughts, feelings, and emotions into captivity, our spirits will remain in a weakened state, completely vulnerable to Satan's attacks.

When our spirits are in a weakened condition, our bodies are weakened, and we begin to live according to the desires of our flesh. We become vulnerable to Satan's attacks on our bodies. We are unable to bear up under trials and physical afflictions. We are unable to resist the sickness and disease Satan tries to place on us, and we are unable to release our faith and believe God for His strength and healing to be manifested in our bodies.

> *The spirit of a man will sustain his infirmity, but a wounded spirit who can bear?*
>
> Proverbs 18:14

We cannot expect to walk in power and victory while our spirits are wounded and in such a weakened condition because of anger, self-pity, bitterness, resentment, and unforgiveness. That is why it is so important, beloved, for you to allow God to perform spiritual surgery on you and heal you of your past wounds.

GOD HAS PLANNED FOR YOU TO EXPERIENCE TOTAL WHOLENESS!

It is God's will that your entire being...spirit, soul, and body...be made TOTALLY WHOLE and BE PRESERVED BLAMELESS until Christ's return. Paul prayed for the believers in the Church in Thessalonica:

> *And the very God of peace sanctify you wholly; and I pray God your whole spirit and soul and body be preserved blameless unto the coming of our Lord Jesus Christ. Faithful is he that calleth you, who also will do it.*
>
> I Thessalonians 5:23-24

Circle the words "wholly" and "whole" in this verse. The word "wholly" is translated from the Greek word *holoteles,* which means "whole, complete...through and through!" Paul prayed that the believers would be wholly sanctified...that the WHOLE man be sanctified in every aspect of his being: spirit...soul...body. He was speaking of the ultimate spiritual maturity God has planned for us, where every aspect of our being is made 100 percent WHOLE and brought into control of God's Spirit within us.

The Greek word for "spirit" is *pneuma.* The *pneuma* of man is the life that God has placed within him to know, communicate with, and worship God. *"God is a spirit: and they that worship Him must worship Him in spirit and in truth"* (John 4:24). It is the life that God breathes into man. God *formeth the spirit of man within him"* (Zechariah 12:1). It is the part of man that is able to comprehend, discern, and understand the things of God.

Paul prayed for the Ephesian church:

> *That the God of our Lord Jesus Christ, the Father of glory, may give unto you the spirit of wisdom and revelation in the knowledge of Him: The eyes of your understanding being enlightened; that ye may know what is the hope of His calling, and what the riches of the glory of His inheritance in the saints.*
>
> Ephesians 1:17-18

In these verses Paul was not praying for the natural mind, with its ability to reason and understand. He was referring to spiritual understanding. The natural mind cannot receive and know the things of God. They are SPIRITUALLY DISCERNED! This is a function of our spirits, not our natural minds.

Paul told the Corinthian believers:

> *Now we have received, not the spirit of the world, but the spirit which is of God; that we might know the things that are freely given to us of God. Which things also we speak, not in the words which man's wisdom teacheth, but which the Holy Ghost teacheth; comparing spiritual things with spiritual. But the natural man receiveth not the things of the Spirit of God: for they are foolishness unto him: neither can he know them, because they are spiritually discerned.*
>
> I Corinthians 2:12-14

Through God's Spirit living within our SPIRITS, we are able to KNOW the things God HAS FREELY GIVEN US!

By His Spirit within us, we have a spirit of revelation and wisdom and are able to discern spiritual truths that are not according to man's wisdom but according to God's!

DO NOT ALLOW YOUR FEELINGS AND EMOTIONS TO RULE OVER YOU!

God has planned that our minds...wills...emotions... feelings...thoughts...desires...and our bodies with their physical appetites...be ROLLED OVER by our spirit man that is controlled by His Spirit within us. Once our spirits are healed and restored and we are living according to the Spirit, our minds and bodies must come into line with the Word of God.

Satan's strategy is to keep you in a weakened position where you are controlled by your feelings and emotions. As long as you allow your emotions and feelings to have free rein and rule over you, you remain vulnerable to Satan's attacks and are unable to walk in the power and victory God has planned for you.

Before you can release the deep hurts of your past and be restored to TOTAL WHOLENESS, you must take authority over your feelings and emotions and bring them into submission to the Holy Spirit living within you. Regardless of how deeply you may have been hurt or how emotionally battered and scarred you may be, you must RELEASE, get-rid of-the feelings you are still holding on to.

By His Spirit living within us, our spirits are strengthened with "ALL MIGHT"...HIS DUNAMIS POWER...which enables us to overcome and be victorious regardless of how deeply we may have been wounded. HOW YOU RESPOND to the deep hurts in your life will determine whether you will live in power and victory or in weakness and defeat.

There are many Christians living in defeat because they are still bound to the past by their FEELINGS and EMOTIONS. Before they can be WHOLE again...set free from their past...restored...healed...they must RELEASE their feelings.

When we experience deep hurts, our feelings are stirred up. Feelings of anger, self-pity, bitterness, resentment, and unforgiveness try to control our actions. If we fail to be honest with ourselves, recognize those feelings, get rid of them, and bring our feelings and emotions into submission, where they are controlled by the Holy Spirit, they will cause deep wounds in our spirits which will keep us in a spiritually weakened condition.

Satan will try to use past hurts to hinder you from walking in the power and victory God has planned for you. Now you are learning HOW TO RELEASE those feelings and receive God's healing for your deep hurts.

It is not the deep hurts we experience that can defeat us, but rather HOW WE REACT TO THEM. How we react determines whether we will become a VICTIM or a VICTOR.

If we react IN THE FLESH and allow our feelings and emotions to control us, we will FROM THE FLESH, reap corruption. We will bring ourselves into an even worse condition and will become a VICTIM, vulnerable to Satan's attacks.

If we react IN THE SPIRIT and take control over our feelings and emotions and bring them under the control of the Holy Spirit living within us, we will FROM THE SPIRIT, reap life. God's life will be released within us. He will heal our wounds and we will rise up a VICTOR!

WE MUST NOT LIVE ACCORDING TO OUR FEELINGS, BUT ACCORDING TO THE WORD OF GOD!

It is time for the Church of Jesus Christ to grow up! Instead of allowing our feelings and emotions to control us, we must rule over them BY GOD'S SPIRIT within us.

Many Christians are continually living in defeat because they are "wearing their feelings on their sleeves." Every time they turn around, they are getting their feelings hurt. Their feelings get hurt over the smallest things...someone says something to them they don't like...the pastor does not recognize the work they have done in the church...someone else is given a position of importance instead of them...another church member treats them badly. They go around whining and complaining about how badly they have been treated, holding bitterness and unforgiveness in their hearts toward those who have hurt them.

It is time for us to STOP LIVING ACCORDING TO OUR FEELINGS! Regardless of how deeply we are hurt...or how often...we must not react according to our flesh, but according to the Spirit of God.

We cannot get the work done God has called us to do if we continue to live according to HOW WE FEEL. It is time for our spirits to rise up (in the dunamis power of God within us) to take authority over our feelings and emotions and bring them into submission to God's Spirit within us.

Paul told the Corinthians:

> *For we walk by faith, not by sight.*
> II Corinthians 5:7

As sons of God, we are no longer bound by the flesh. The spirit rules over our souls and bodies.

It doesn't matter HOW WE FEEL...we no longer live according to HOW WE FEEL, what we see or do not see, but we live and act according to the Spirit.

It doesn't matter HOW WE FEEL...we act according to God's Word!

As long as we live, we will be subject to deep hurts, disappointments, and mistreatment. We will be wounded, hated, persecuted, rejected, and suffer affliction, but we will always be victorious when we act according to the Spirit.

RECOGNIZE THE FEELINGS AND EMOTIONS THAT ARE TRYING TO TAKE HOLD!

To receive healing and live in victory over the deep hurts in your life, the first step you must take is to RECOGNIZE the feelings and emotions that are trying to take hold in your life. The very moment you are mistreated...hurt...wounded... choose to be a VICTOR...not a victim. Refuse to react in the flesh. Refuse to give Satan an opportunity to gain a stronghold in your life. Paul told the Romans:

> *But put ye on the Lord Jesus Christ, and make not provisions for the flesh, to fulfill the lust thereof.*
> Romans 13:14

Don't make any provision or allowances for your flesh to react in anger, self-pity, bitterness, resentment, unforgiveness or revenge toward those who have hurt you. Put a stop to the flesh by taking control of your feelings and emotions. You may FEEL like lashing out in anger. You may FEEL unforgiving. You may FEEL like holding a grudge. Don't do it! Don't give in to your flesh.

God does not expect us to deny or ignore our feelings and emotions. It is natural to have them, but we do not have to allow them to control us! There are many Christians today who have experienced deep hurts, but they have failed to recognize and deal directly with their feelings. They are afraid that if they acknowledge they have been hurt or honestly express their true feelings, other Christians will think it is a lack of faith on their part or a "bad confession."

So they hide their deep hurts behind a mask. They are smiling on the outside...PRETENDING to be victorious...but hurting on the inside, not knowing what to do and how to be healed and restored. They are like a time bomb walking around ready to explode at any moment.

Because of various teachings within the Church in recent years, there are many who believe that Christians should always have a smile on their faces, always be spiritually "up"...never have any problems...and if they do have problems, it is because their faith is weak. As a result, many Christians have tried to deny or ignore their feelings because of fear of what other Christians will say to them.

They are PRETENDING they are not hurting... PRETENDING they are not depressed or discouraged... PRETENDING they are walking in faith and victory, when they actually desperately need to be set free from the past and healed of their deep wounds.

On the outside they are smiling...but deep down they are full of despair and hopelessness. They are ready to give up and many are so miserable they are trying to find a way to take their own lives. I'm not talking about the unsaved. I'm talking about men and women who have been born again...faithful members in our churches.

It is time to take the mask off, to stop the pretending and to deal directly, openly, and honestly before God with the feelings and deep hurts in our lives!

God has made full provision for us to experience healing, where we can be WHOLE...spirit...soul...body. God's promise to us today is,

> *For I will restore health unto thee, and I will heal thee of the wounds, saith the Lord.*
>
> Jeremiah 30:17

Before we can experience healing of our deep hurts, we must be totally honest with ourselves and with God, recognize our feelings and deal with them IN THE SPIRIT!

CONFESS YOUR FEELINGS TO GOD!

The second step you must take to receive God's healing for your deep hurts is to confess your feelings to God. Pour out your feelings to Him. He is the only One Who can heal your wounded spirit.

If you are holding on to feelings of anger, resentment, or bitterness toward someone who has hurt you in the past...an unfaithful husband or wife...a rebellious child...an abusive parent...an employer...a pastor...another member of the Body of Christ...confess it openly before God.

It may be that you have become angry or bitter toward God because of circumstances, sickness, and tragedies you have experienced, or because you have not received an answer to your prayers. Don't try to hide your feelings from God. He knows your innermost feelings and thoughts. Don't give Satan an opportunity to gain a stronghold in your life by going around murmuring and complaining, speaking words against God or against those who have hurt you from the bitterness of your spirit.

Open your spirit wide and pour out your feelings to Him. Ask God to forgive you for holding these feelings in your spirit and to give you power through the Holy Spirit to get rid of them.

Don't be afraid or ashamed to confess your true feelings to the Lord. Christ, Who is our High Priest, knows your feelings and is touched with the feeling of your infirmities.

> *For we do not have a High Priest Who is unable to sympathize and have a shared feeling with our weaknesses and infirmities and liability to the assaults of temptation, but One Who has been tempted in every respect as we are, yet without sinning. Let us then fearlessly and confidently and boldly draw near to the throne of grace (the throne of God's unmerited favor to us sinners) that we may receive mercy [for our failures] and find grace to help in good time for every need [appropriate help and well-timed help, coming just when we need it].*
>
> Hebrews 4:15-16 AMP

You must come to Him BOLDLY, without fear, knowing that He will be merciful and give you the strength and grace to release any feelings of bitterness, resentment, anger, or unforgiveness you are still holding on to.

RELEASE YOUR FEELINGS OF ANGER, BITTERNESS, RESENTMENT, SELF-PITY AND UNFORGIVENESS!

The third step to receive God's healing for your deep hurts is to RELEASE...get rid of your feelings of anger, bitterness, resentment, self-pity, and unforgiveness. The moment you are hurt deeply by someone, or by the circumstances, burdens, and infirmities Satan brings into your life, you must decide at that moment whether you will allow your feelings and emotions to control you and become a VICTIM, or whether you will take control of your feelings and bring them into submission of the Holy Spirit and become a VICTOR.

When you are hurt, you must decide whether or not you will continue to hold on to your feelings of anger, bitterness, resentment, self-pity, and unforgiveness and be bound to your past, or to release them and allow God to heal you and make you EVERY WHIT WHOLE.

Know that God has planned for your spirits to rule over your soul...mind...will...FEELINGS...EMOTIONS...and your body with its physical desires, and that He has placed His Spirit within you, giving you His dunamis power. You must rise up in the Spirit and take authority over your feelings.

If you are holding feelings of anger toward the person who has hurt you, you must take authority over it and GET RID OF IT! Paul told the Ephesians:

> *Get rid of all bitterness, rage and anger, brawling and slander, along with every form of malice. Be kind and compassionate to one another, forgiving each other, just as in Christ God forgave you.*
> Ephesians 4:31-32 NIV

By the Spirit of God that is within you, GET RID OF THEM! If you are holding feelings of bitterness, self-pity, resentment, or unforgiveness, GET RID OF THEM! You may not feel like forgiving or getting rid of a grudge you are holding against someone who has hurt you deeply...you may not feel like releasing bitterness...you may feel you are justified in bitterness because of what the other has done to hurt you.

It does not matter how you FEEL! If you are a true son of God filled with His Spirit, you are no longer bound or controlled by your feelings. As an act of your will, RELEASE the anger. As an act of your will, RELEASE the bitterness. As an act of your will, RELEASE the resentment. As an act of your will, RELEASE the self-pity. As an act of your will, RELEASE the unforgiveness.

You may have been hurt so deeply you feel you can not ever forgive the one who has hurt you. Confess how you feel to God. Ask Him, "Forgive me for the unforgiveness I have had in my spirit toward the people who have hurt me. Forgive me of the anger, bitterness, resentment, or hatred. I am willing to forgive, even though I don't feel like it. As an act of my will, I release this unforgiveness toward them. Let Your forgiveness and love flow through me."

After you have released the feelings you have had in your spirit toward those who have hurt you, go to them and confess the feelings you have had toward them and ask their forgiveness. Be reconciled into fellowship with them.

COMMIT YOURSELF TO GOD!

The fourth step in receiving God's healing for your deep hurts is to simply COMMIT YOURSELF TO God and trust Him to heal and restore you. After you have released all feelings you have had in your spirit toward those who have hurt you, YOU WILL BE SET FREE FROM THE PAST. Regardless of whether or not the other person is willing to be reconciled to you, you will no longer be bound to them or your past hurts.

Just as Christ suffered and refused to react in the flesh to take revenge, but willingly forgave those who rejected, despised, slandered, mercilessly beat, and crucified Him, and submitted Himself into the hands of God, we are to do the same.

> *...Christ also suffered for us, leaving us an example, that ye should follow his steps: Who did no sin, neither was guile found in His mouth: Who, when He was reviled, reviled not again; when He suffered, He threatened not; but committed Himself to Him that judgeth righteously.*
>
> I Peter 2:21-23

After you have taken authority over your feelings and brought them into submission to the Holy Spirit, and have done everything possible to be reconciled to those who have hurt you, you must then COMMIT yourself into the hands of God and trust Him to complete the healing and restoration in your life.

As you commit yourself into His hands, you must trust Him to cleanse and remove every trace of anger, bitterness, resentment, self-pity, and unforgiveness that you may have had in your spirit.

You must release your faith and take hold of His promise of healing:

> *For I will restore health unto thee, and I will heal thee of thy wounds, saith the Lord...*
>
> Jeremiah 30:17

Faith is a fact, but faith is an act! Regardless of how you may FEEL, you must act on God's promise of healing and receive it into your spirit. Believe it and walk in that healing. As you do, Christ will pour in the oil and wine of the Holy Spirit into your deep hurts and heal you!

Say aloud: "God has planned for me to experience TOTAL WHOLENESS...spirit...soul...body...where I am continually being healed, continually being restored, continually being strengthened by His Spirit living within me!"

TAKE THE LIMITS OFF GOD!

Beloved, like the waters in the pool of Bethesda which were troubled by the angel, the waters of the Spirit are troubled. God is bringing healing and restoration to the Body of Christ.

Do you want to be made WHOLE...spirit...soul...body? Just as Jesus asked the man who had an infirmity for 38 years, "Wilt thou be made whole?" He is asking you today:

"Will you be made WHOLE...spirit, soul, body? Will you reach out in faith to receive My provision of healing for all your needs? Will you dare to believe Me and walk in new strength and victory?

"This is the day I am restoring my Body to a new position of strength, power and total wholeness. Hear My voice. Receive My healing.

"Reach out your hand and touch My bleeding side. Feel the wounds in My hands. See the stripes and scars that I carry in My body for you. They are sufficient for ALL pain, sickness, heartache...for ALL ages...for ALL time.

"Receive healing for the deep hurts in your life. I came to set you free. Don't hold on to the past. Don't refuse My provision of healing for you. Take it now!

"Be healed in your spirit! Be healed and restored in your soul! Be healed and set free of every pain and sickness in your body!"

CHAPTER SIX

Receive the Word of the Lord into your spirit and act on it right now. Stretch your hands up to the Lord and claim whatever you need. While the spirit of the Lord is upon you, release the heavy load you are carrying. Let the Lord pour the oil and the wine of the Holy Spirit into your wounds and pour new strength into your spirit, soul, and body. TO WALK IN TOTAL WHOLENESS, YOU MUST TAKE CONTROL OF YOUR FEELINGS AND EMOTIONS!

To be healed of the deep hurts of your past and walk in the TOTAL WHOLENESS God has provided for you, you must go beyond the surface out onto the battlefield of your soul and take control of your FEELINGS and EMOTIONS. Until you learn how to bring them into submission and under the control of the Holy Spirit, you will continually face one defeat after another. You will be up one day and down the next. Your strength will fluctuate with your emotions and your actions will be based upon how you FEEL instead of what God has promised in His Word!

Satan has gained a major stronghold in the lives of many Christians today, because they are living their life ACCORDING TO THEIR FEELINGS. They are ruled by their feelings and emotions. They base their actions on HOW THEY FEEL instead of what the Word of God says.

God has placed His Spirit within us and has planned that our souls and bodies be regulated and controlled by His Spirit...NOT by our FEELINGS or the dictates of our flesh.

Our spirits, which have been infused and empowered by the dunamis power of God, are to RULE over our souls and bodies. We are to live our lives according to the Spirit of God within us.

Paul told the Galatians:

> *But I say, walk and live [habitually] in the [Holy] Spirit*
> *[responsive to and controlled and guided by the Spirit];*
> *then you will certainly not gratify the cravings and*
> *desires of the flesh (of human nature without God). For*
> *the desires of the flesh are opposed to the [Holy] Spirit,*
> *and the [desires of the] Spirit are opposed to the flesh*
> *(godless human nature); for these are antagonistic to*
> *each other [continually withstanding and in conflict with*
> *each other] so that you are not free but are prevented*
> *from doing what you desire to do.*
>
> Galatians 5:16-17 AMP

Paul told the Romans:

> *...Sending His own Son in the guise of sinful flesh and*
> *as an offering for sin, [God] condemned sin in the flesh*
> *[subdued, overcame, deprived it of its power over all*
> *who accept that sacrifice]. So that the righteous and just*
> *requirement of the Law might be fully met in us, who*
> *live and move not in the ways of the flesh but in the*
> *ways of the Spirit [our lives governed not by the*
> *standards and according to the dictates of the flesh, but*
> *controlled by the Holy Spirit].*
>
> Romans 8:3-4 AMP

The power of sin has been broken over us; and if the Spirit of God DWELLS in our spirits, we are no longer to live according to our "flesh"...which is according to our foolish nature and desires of our bodies.

Paul said:

> *For those who are according to the flesh and are*
> *controlled by its unholy desires, set their minds on and*
> *pursue those things which gratify the flesh. But those*

105

> *who are according to the Spirit and are controlled by the desires of the spirit, set their minds on and seek those things which gratify the [Holy] Spirit.*
>
> Romans 8:5 AMP

There is no middle ground! If we truly have God's Spirit living within us...controlling every aspect of our beings...we will not live the life of the flesh. We will not be ruled and controlled by our emotions or feelings!

Paul told the Romans:

> *But you are not living the life of the flesh, you are living the life of the Spirit, if the [Holy] Spirit of God [really] dwells within you [directs and controls you].*
>
> Romans 8:9 AMP

Paul said that IF the Holy Spirit of God is dwelling within us, directing and controlling our lives, we will not live a life of the flesh. Do not be deceived! There is no such thing as a "carnal" Christian. If the Holy Spirit is in us, directing and controlling our lives, we will be living according to the Spirit. Paul said, *"...But if any one does not possess the [Holy] Spirit of Christ, he is none of His [he does not belong to Christ, is not truly a child of God]"* (Romans 8:9 AMP).

It is *"those who are led by the Spirit of God who are the sons of God"* (Romans 8:14). Not everyone professing to be a son of God is a true son of God. Here is the test: Those who have the Holy Spirit dwelling within them and who are walking according to the Spirit...controlled and directed by Him...are the sons of God.

OUR SPIRITS ARE TO RULE OVER OUR SOULS AND BODIES!

Jesus paid the ultimate price. He offered Himself up as a sacrifice so that the power of sin over us would be broken and we would no longer be controlled by our flesh. We owe a debt! Our lives are no longer our own to live according to our desires, to please ourselves.

Paul said:

> *So then, brethren, we are debtors, but not to the flesh [we are not obligated to our carnal nature] to live [a life ruled by the standards set up by the dictates] of the flesh. For if you live according to [the dictates of] the flesh you will surely die. But if through the power of the [Holy] Spirit you are [habitually] putting to death (making extinct, deadening the) [evil] deeds prompted by the body, you shall [really and genuinely] live forever.*
>
> Romans 8:12-13 AMP

He told the Galatians:

> *But I say, walk and live [habitually] in the [Holy] Spirit responsive to and controlled and guided by the Spirit; then you will certainly not gratify the cravings and desires of the flesh of human nature without God.*
>
> Galatians 5:16 AMP

Our responsibility before God is to rule over our souls and bodies through the dunamis power of the Holy Spirit within our spirits, by putting to death the cravings and desires of the flesh. Paul said:

> *And they that are Christ's have crucified the flesh with the affections and lust.*
>
> Galatians 5:24

One of the major reasons there are so many Christians who are still holding on to the hurts of the past and who are in a spiritually weakened condition and so vulnerable to Satan's attacks, is because they are still living according to the dictates and desires of their flesh. As a result, they are bringing destruction upon both their souls and bodies.

Paul warned the Galatians:

> *Do not be deceived and deluded and misled; God will not allow Himself to be sneered at (scorned, disdained or mocked by mere pretensions or professions, or by His precepts being set aside). [He inevitably deludes himself who attempts to delude God]. For whatever a man sows, that and that only is what he will reap. For he who sows his own flesh (lower nature, sensuality) will from the flesh reap decay and ruin and destruction, but he who sows to the Spirit will from the Spirit reap life eternal.*
>
> Galatians 6:7-8 AMP

Christians who are still living according to the flesh and allowing their souls...minds, thoughts, wills, emotions, feelings...to control them, are bringing death and destruction upon themselves. They have deceived themselves into thinking they can have God's blessings upon their lives while they are still living sensual lives...fulfilling the lust and cravings of their flesh.

BREAK THE CHAINS OF THE PAST!

One of the major strategies Satan is using today to weaken and hinder the Church from taking its position of power God has planned for us in this end-time harvest, is to keep the past before us as a stumbling block.

He has been digging up the past sins and failures of Christian leaders and ministries and has been throwing them in our face to discredit the Church in the eyes of the world and to shake the faith of Christians.

The time has come for the Church of Jesus Christ to break the chains of the past and LET THE HEALING BEGIN!

It is time for us to put the past failures, the past hurts, and the past sins of recent years behind us and take hold of all that God has planned for us in this Decade of Destiny!

God is saying to us:

"It's time to draw a line on the past. There is no time to look back. Get your eyes set on the goal that I have placed before you. The past will keep you in bondage. The past will hold you back from fulfilling the work I have called you to do. Forget the past and take my hand. The greatest victories are on the horizon. Let go of the past and receive a new vision of what lies ahead for My people in this hour. Don't look to the past...look to me. Commit the past into My hands and I will lead you to victory after victory."

God wants you to be made WHOLE...spirit...soul...body. He wants to set you free from the past. Jesus came to HEAL THE BROKENHEARTED! He came to preach DELIVERANCE TO THE CAPTIVES! He came to SET AT LIBERTY THOSE WHO ARE BRUISED!

Jesus was anointed by the Holy Spirit and with power; He was sent to HEAL and SET FREE those who would have been crushed, those who are bruised, broken, and bleeding from deep hurts by the problems, trials, and tragedies they have experienced in their lives.

If you allow him to, Satan will keep you chained to your past by the hurts, disappointments, and failures you have experienced. He will keep you in bondage to the painful memories, the deep-rooted feelings, the guilt of past sins you have committed. He will torment you by continually bringing up your past failures and will remind you of your weaknesses to keep you from attaining the fullness of what God has for you.

Satan is a liar! He has lied to many Christians and convinced them that because of their past sins and failures, God's plan for their lives has changed and that He will no longer use them as He had planned...that they are limited in how God will use them. They believe they are forgiven, but they are convinced that, because of all that has happened in the past, they are unworthy or incapable of being used by God to accomplish His work today.

There are Christians who are chained to the past by the hurts, disappointments, and failures they have experienced. They are no longer looking, expecting, or believing God to fulfill His purpose in their lives. They have lost sight of the vision God has given them of what He wants to accomplish through them. They are afraid to reach out and take hold of God's promises. They have limited what God can do in their lives.

Satan is keeping many Christians chained to the past through guilt and condemnation over past sins. They are weighed down by guilt for sins they have already confessed and continue to beat themselves down emotionally and mentally over them.

YOU CAN BE SET FREE FROM YOUR PAST!

Regardless of all the pain and confusion, sin and failures you may have experienced in your life...

You can be SET FREE from your past! Jesus came for this purpose! He came to SET AT LIBERTY those who are bruised. Don't listen to Satan's lies. There is healing for your memories! There is healing of your deep hurts! There is healing for your emotions! You can let go of the past and be set free to experience TOTAL WHOLENESS in your life!

Your past is over...dead...buried! Your past, including the pain, hurts, disappointments, sins, and defeats has already been nailed to the cross. It is already gone!

Before you can be totally healed and restored, you must, by faith, RELEASE your past. By "releasing your past," I am not talking about repressing your memories or trying to cover them up and putting them in the back of your mind.

I am not talking about PRETENDING they are gone or trying to ignore them.

I am not talking about psychology trying to explain them away.

To release your past, you must first get rid of the feelings that bind you to the past...anger, resentment, bitterness, hatred, unforgiveness, self-pity, and any other negative feelings. As you learned in last week's lesson, you must take authority over your feelings and emotions and bring them into submission with the Holy Spirit.

Then you must bring your past, with its sin, hurts, disappointments, and failures to the cross and consider it buried with Christ. Through the one perfect sacrifice of His own life, Christ condemned sin and set us free from its bondage, including our past. We are dead to sin. The past is dead and buried, and we are set free to live the life of the Spirit.

111

Paul told the Romans:

> *Sending His own Son in the guise of sinful flesh as an offering for sin, [God] condemned sin in the flesh [subdued, overcame, deprived of its power over all who accept the sacrifice].*
>
> Romans 8:3 AMP

The power of sin over our lives has been broken, and we are to consider our bodies dead to sin...our relationship to it ended...and that our spirits are alive to God.

> *[Jesus] Who his own self bare our sins in his own body on the tree, that we, being dead to sins, should live unto righteousness: by whose stripes ye were healed.*
>
> I Peter 2:24

Paul told the Romans:

> *For by the death He died, He died to sin [ending His relation to it] once for all, and the life that He lives, He is living to God [in unbroken fellowship with Him]. Even so consider yourself also dead to sin and your relation to it broken, but alive to God [living in unbroken fellowship with Him] in Christ Jesus.*
>
> Romans 6:10-11 AMP

Not only are we dead to sin, but through Christ, the past with its sins, hurts, and brokenness is gone, dead, CRUCIFIED! The past is dead and regardless of what you have experienced in the past, Christ has made FULL PROVISION for TOTAL HEALING...not only for your salvation but He has set you free from the bondage of the past. — DRAW A LINE ON THE PAST! —

Knowing that the past is dead, you must draw a line on it. FORGET IT...put it behind you and refuse to allow Satan to bring it up any more. Stop listening to the lies. If there are past hurts, sins, or failures that Satan is trying to use against you, you need to bury them, take hold of the future and DON'T LOOK BACK!

Refuse to hold onto the past! Satan will use your past hurts, sins, and failures to drag you down...to keep you from experiencing the fullness of God's blessings. Don't allow your mind to dwell on the past. Bring your thoughts, feelings, and emotions into control of the Holy Spirit. You CAN do it! WALK in the Spirit, with your spirit controlling your soul and body! Forget what is behind you and set your eyes to the victory God has set you before you.

Paul told the Philippians:

> *I do not consider, brethren, that I have captured and made it my own [yet]; but one thing I do it [is my one aspiration]: forgetting what lies behind and straining forward to what lies ahead, I press on toward the goal to win the [supreme and heavenly] prize to which God in Christ Jesus is calling us upward.*
>
> Philippians 3:13-14 AMP

Paul had drawn a line on the past. Before his conversion on the road to Damascus, he had been an archenemy of the Church. He had persecuted and brought men and women, bound, into prison and had participated in Stephen's death. He said:

> *And I persecuted this way unto the death, binding and delivering into prisons both men and women.*
>
> Acts 22:4

After his conversion, he made a 180 degree turn and God used him mightily to build and strengthen the Church he once set out to destroy. Throughout his ministry, he had experienced many great victories...signs and wonders had been manifested...churches established...multitudes of Gentiles converted. He had faced hardships...suffered hunger...been slandered...beaten...stoned...imprisoned. But he refused to hold on to the past.

Paul said, *"...but this one thing I do..."* He had focused his attention on one objective. He did not allow his past or disappointments to distract him. This one purpose dominated his whole life and conduct.

He said, *"forgetting what lies behind..."* In these verses he was not talking about a one-time experience of shutting out the past with its guilt, condemnation, and painful memories, Paul was referring to a CONTINUAL FORGETTING...a CONTINUAL EFFORT of putting the past behind him and centering all his energies and interest on the cause set before him. He was talking about a CONTINUAL REFUSAL to let the past weigh him down and stop his progress.

We know that our past sins have been crucified with Christ and that our past failures, hurts, and disappointments are behind us. But Satan will keep bombarding our minds with thoughts of the past until we are distracted and unable to concentrate on the vision and course God has set before us.

Satan's objective is to get us to keep living in the past... thinking about what might have been...full of self-condemnation and guilt...discouraged and beaten down by past failures. He wants the past to thus dominate and control our minds until we are SPIRITUALLY PARALYZED.

WHEN SATAN BRINGS UP THE PAST, REFUSE IT!

To break the chains of the past and be set free from the painful memories of past hurts, we must put forth a conscious effort to forget. There are times when we have a desire to forget and forgive those who have hurt us and get on with our lives, but it seems we just cannot do it. Our feelings and emotions keep us tied to the past. That is why it is so important that we begin to take authority over our feelings and emotions and bring them into submission to the Holy Spirit.

We try to shut out the pain...to forget our memories and put them out of our minds once and for all. But Satan will come to stir it all up, and will try to use the past to torment us and keep us in a weakened position.

To be set free from the past, you must continually REFUSE to allow Satan to use your past to defeat you. Through the power of the Holy Spirit that lives within you, God has made it possible for your SPIRIT to rule over your soul and body.

Through the power of the Holy Spirit, REFUSE to allow your mind to dwell on the past. When Satan brings up the past, REFUSE it! Use your power and authority to reject it and bring your thoughts into submission to the Holy Spirit.

Paul told the Corinthians:

> *For the weapons of our warfare are not carnal, but mighty through God to the pulling down of strong holds; Casting down imaginations, and every high thing that exalteth itself against the knowledge of God, and bringing into captivity every thought to the obedience of Christ.*

> II Corinthians 10:4-5

115

You have the power and authority through the Holy Spirit to keep the past behind you. You don't have to allow the hurts, failures, and sins of the past to rule over you. To break the chains of the past, you must continually bring your thoughts into captivity and REFUSE to be distracted and hindered by the past.

To be set free from the past, you must not only concentrate on keeping the past behind you, but you must CHANGE YOUR FOCUS. Instead of allowing your mind to dwell on the past...nursing old wounds...filled with bitterness...filled with condemnation and guilt over past failures...you must set your eyes on the goal God has set before you and focus all your attention and energies on fulfilling the work God has called you to do.

Paul said, *"forgetting what lies behind and straining forward to what lies ahead."* In the King James translation it reads, *"reaching forth unto those things which are before."* The Greek word used to translate "reaching forth" refers to an athlete in a race who throws himself forward with all his energies, straining to the very utmost toward the goal.

In these verses Paul compared our lives to an athlete running in a race, with his face set like a flint to finish the race and WIN THE PRIZE. Not only are we to make a conscious effort to continually keep the past behind us, we must put forth every effort and concentrate all our energies on fulfilling the work God has given us to do.

Beloved, it's time to get serious!

We don't have time to look back at our past sins and failures!

We don't have time to keep holding on to our past hurts!

We don't have time to waste our energy whining, complaining, or worrying about the past!

WE MUST FORGET WHAT IS BEHIND AND SPIRITUALLY STRIVE TOWARD THE GOAL BEFORE US!

In a race, the runner does not look behind him, but keeps his eyes fixed on the course and the goal until he reaches it and crosses the finish line. If he continually kept glancing back over his shoulder, focusing his attention on the course he had run or his opponents, he would be distracted from his objective of winning the race. He would lose time and could stumble or get off course.

What Paul was talking about in these verses was SPIRITUAL STRIVING...SPIRITUAL FORTITUDE and SPIRITUAL PERSEVERANCE! Like a runner in a race, we are to forget what is behind us and SPIRITUALLY STRIVE...STRAIN...FOCUS ALL OF OUR CONCENTRATION...EXERT ALL OUR ENERGY...on the goal that is set before us!

Paul said, *"I press toward the mark for the prize of the high calling of God in Christ Jesus"* (Philippians 3:14). He was in hot pursuit! He refused to become distracted or slowed down by the past.

It is time for the Church of Jesus Christ to get spiritually violent! Jesus said:

> And from the days of John the Baptist until the present time the kingdom of heaven has endured violent assault, and violent men seize it by force [as a precious prize – a share in the heavenly kingdom is sought with most ardent zeal and intense exertion].
>
> Matthew 11:12 AMP

117

Instead of yielding to the opposition of the enemy and getting our eyes on the past instead of the future, of what God is bringing us into in this end time hour, we must SPIRITUALLY STRIVE "with most ardent zeal and intense exertion" to accomplish the work God has given us. We must concentrate our energies on the future and PRESS on in hot pursuit!

We must spiritually strive, not according to our own limited natural strength, but in the power of HIS MIGHT! Paul said:

> ...I labor, striving according to His power, which mightily works within me.
> Colossians 1:29 NAS

Through His dunamis, miracle-working power that is working within our spirits, we are to draw from His immeasurable, inexhaustible supply of strength and exert all our energy in forgetting the past and taking hold of all that God has for us.

This is the message that God has for His Church today! God is bringing healing and restoration to the Church. It is time for us to bury the past failures, and sins of recent years that Satan has been using to slow us down and hinder the progress we have been making in pulling down his strongholds in the nations of the world.

The past is dead...gone! We must REFUSE to allow Satan to use it against us. When he brings up the past, we must reject it and keep pressing forward in accomplishing God's purposes. Beloved, we are heading down the home stretch.

We are living in the Decade of Destiny where the Church is going to rise up in greater power and victory than ever before to fulfill His end-time plan. We cannot afford to look back or hold on to the past.

It is time to draw a line on the past and DON'T LOOK BACK!

In your own life, what are the past hurts, sins, failures, and disappointments Satan is using to keep you chained to your past?

Are you SPIRITUALLY STRIVING...exerting all your energy on the goal that God has set before you?

Are you still bound to the past because of feelings of hatred, bitterness, resentment, or unforgiveness?

Are you still looking back at past sins and failures and limiting God? Are there painful memories from the past that need to be healed in your life?

You can be set free today! You don't have to keep carrying your past around with you. Jesus came to SET AT LIBERTY those who are bruised, shattered, broken. You must recognize that your past, with it's sins, hurts failures, and brokenness, is gone...dead...crucified. By faith you must bring those things of the past and bury them. Release them from your life and refuse to allow Satan to use them against you.

BREAK THE CHAINS OF CONDEMNATION AND GUILT FROM THE PAST!

There are many Christians who are chained to the past by guilt and condemnation over past sins and failures. Satan is beating them down and making them feel guilty over sins that have been confessed and forgiven by God years and years ago.

Are there memories of past sins and failures that are holding you back from feeling forgiven and loved by God? Are there sins from your past that Satan is using to make you feel God cannot use you?

God wants you to know that the past sin that has been weighing you down has been put to death... crucified on the cross of Jesus Christ...never to be remembered any more! If you have sincerely repented of your sin and yet you are still carrying a burden of guilt for the past, it is a needless burden you carry; and it is time for you to get rid of it and break the chains of the past.

There are many Christians living in defeat who are looking back at their sins of the past...their failures and weaknesses, who have accepted the fact they will just have to live with the pain of the guilt and the memory of their sin. They have never been able to RELEASE or let go of the shame and guilt they have carried.

CHAPTER SEVEN

If you are still living under guilt and condemnation over past sins, Christ wants to set you free and make you totally WHOLE again. As a child of God, you don't have to listen to the lies and accusations of Satan concerning your past sins. While you were still dead in your sins, your past was forgiven along with your sins. Paul told the Ephesians:

> But God, being rich in mercy, because of His great love with which He loved us, even when we were dead in our transgressions, made us alive together with Christ (by grace you have been saved), and raised us up with Him, and seated us with Him in the heavenly places, in Christ Jesus.
>
> Ephesians 2:4-6 NAS

Not only did God completely forgive you of your sins, He wiped the slate clean. Your sins and your past were forgotten. David declared, *"As far as the east is from the west, so far hath he removed our transgressions from the us"* (Psalm 103:12).

God spoke through Isaiah:

> I have blotted out as a thick cloud your transgressions, and like a cloud your sins. Return to Me, for I have redeemed you.
>
> Isaiah 44:22 AMP

He has declared, *"Their sins and their lawless deeds I will remember no more"* (Hebrews 10:17 NAS).

Knowing that the sins of your past have been forever removed and forgotten...that your past is dead...you must put it behind you and move out in faith to take hold of what God has for you. When Satan comes to try to dig up the past and put guilt and condemnation on you, resist him in the Name of Jesus. Refuse to allow him to use your past sins or failures to hinder or stop you from walking in the power and victory God has planned for you.

There will always be people who will try to make you feel guilty...who will continue to bring up your past. There will always be self-appointed judges who will point their fingers and criticize. But when you know that through Christ you are accepted, forgiven, and righteous in God's sight, it won't matter what anyone else says. You will be set free from your past.

Knowing that you are set free from your past...from your hurts...from past sins and failures...you must draw a line on the past and not look back. When Satan tries to bring it up again, you must stop him in his tracks by taking authority over your thoughts and feelings and bring them into submission to the Holy Spirit.

YOU HAVE BEEN SET FREE FROM YOUR PAST!

Regardless of the chains that are binding you to the past, you can be set free today. If you are still carrying hurts from your past...if you are still bound to the past by your feelings...RELEASE them! Come boldly before the Lord with love and confidence. One by one, confess any anger, bitterness, hatred, resentment, or unforgiveness you may still be holding onto concerning those who have hurt you. By faith, see them buried with Christ, never to be remembered.

If there are past sins which you have confessed but for which you have been unable to forgive yourself, or if you have been living in defeat over some sin in your life that you have been struggling to overcome, draw a line on the past and allow the Lord to set you free. There is nothing beyond the power of His love, grace, and mercy to forgive. He will set you free from the past...free from the condemnation and guilt, and will heal and restore you completely.

The great King David committed adultery with Bathsheba and was guilty of arranging the death of her husband, Uriah. Yet God freely forgave him of his sins and set him free of his past. God did not hold his past against him, but continued to use him for His glory.

When David was confronted by Nathan regarding his sin, he recognized and confessed his sin. *"I have sinned against the Lord"* (II Samuel 12:13, AMP). At his confession and repentance, God freely forgave him. Nathan told David:

> *The Lord also has put away your sin; you shall not die.*
> *Nevertheless, because by this deed you have utterly scorned*
> *the Lord and given great occasion to the enemies of the Lord*
> *to blaspheme, the child that is born to you shall surely die.*
> II Samuel 12:13-14 AMP

Although David was forgiven, he reaped the consequences of his sin. Do not be deceived. When we sow the flesh, we will, from the flesh, reap corruption.

David pleaded with God for his son's life. He fasted and lay upon the ground. On the seventh day the child died. When David knew his son was dead, he got up, bathed, dressed, and went into the House of the Lord to worship. He drew a line on the past, put his sin behind him, accepted God's forgiveness, and moved on to serve God in complete restoration. He did not allow his past to stop him from fulfilling the work God had given him as king over Israel.

Regardless of what your past may be, draw a line on it, as David did. Jesus has broken the condemnation of your past sins by offering Himself once and for all. He will forgive you, set you free from your past, and restore you to WHOLENESS.

Having been set free from sin, you are set free from the results of sin: condemnation and death.

Paul told the Romans:

> *There is therefore now no condemnation to them which are in Christ Jesus, who walk not after the flesh, but after the Spirit. For the law of the Spirit of life in Christ Jesus hath made me free from the law of sin and death.*
> Romans 8:1-2

Say aloud: "No condemnation!"

You are SET FREE from your past...FREE from your condemnation and guilt...FREE from the power of sin!

Paul said:

> *Who shall bring any charge against God's elect (when it is) God Who justifies Who puts us in right relation to Himself? (Who shall come forward and accuse or impeach those whom God has chosen? Will God, who acquits us?) Who is there to condemn (us)? Will Christ Jesus, the Messiah, Who died, or rather Who was raised from the dead, Who is at the right hand of God actually pleading as He intercedes for us?*
> Romans 8:33-34 AMP

Praise God! Since God has justified us, there is no reason why you should remain bound to the past with its sins, hurts, failures, condemnation, or guilt. Having been set free, you must put the past behind you...PUT AN END TO IT! Set your eyes on the future God has planned for you in this end-time hour and walk in that freedom. Refuse to allow Satan to bring up your past and use it to defeat you.

Right now, by faith in what Christ has already done for you, begin to release the past. Release the hurts, the painful memories! Release the fear, condemnation, and guilt! Release the failures and sins of the past!

RELEASE YOUR DEEP HURTS AND BE MADE 100 PERCENT WHOLE...SPIRIT...SOUL...BODY!

God is bringing healing and restoration to the Body of Christ! He is pouring in new strength and bringing the Body into a new dimension of spiritual maturity whereby we will experience TOTAL WHOLENESS...SPIRIT...SOUL...BODY!

He is exposing, purging, and cleansing out the sin that has infiltrated and spread throughout the Body, and He is pouring the healing oil of the Holy Spirit into the deep wounds of those who have been battered, crushed, and wounded deeply in their spirits.

He is canceling out the past, and is bringing us into a totally new position of holiness, maturity, spiritual understanding, wisdom, and power far greater than we have ever experienced!

This is a time of RELEASE for the Body of Christ. It is a time of RELEASING the past with all its sins, failures, disappointments, heartaches, and deep hurts. This RELEASE must take place in our lives before we can be healed, restored, and made 100 percent WHOLE.

It is time for those whose lives have been crushed and broken through the pain of separation and divorce to

RELEASE their deep hurts of rejection, anger, bitterness, and unforgiveness.

It is time for parents whose hearts have been battered and bruised by a rebellious son or daughter who has turned away from God and become entangled by sin...drugs...illicit sex, to RELEASE the pain and heartache and receive healing and new strength.

It is time for us who have been carrying deep hurts and have been healed, to RELEASE them and be set free and made whole.

It is time for the Body of Christ, as a whole, to RELEASE the past sins and failures that Satan has been using against us and be healed and restored to a new position of strength.

It is time for the Body of Christ to RELEASE our hurts, to get rid of all the bitterness and unforgiveness toward other members who have hurt us, and be restored into fellowship and a new covenant relationship of God's grace, love, and forgiveness.

Take time right now to think about the deep hurts in your life: the brokenness and pain, the guilt, shame and condemnation over past sins. Think about the pain of rejection, the loss of self-esteem, the heartache you have carried deep within your spirit.

Are you still holding anger, resentment, and unforgiveness toward those who have hurt you? Have you allowed a root of rebellion and bitterness to take hold in your spirit?

Beloved, it is time to RELEASE...to get rid of these things and be set free and made whole!

God's message to us today is:

For I will restore health unto thee, and I will heal thee of thy wounds, saith the LORD...

Jeremiah 30:17

David declared:

He heals the brokenhearted and binds up their wounds, curing their pains and their sorrows.

Psalm 147:3 AMP

Jesus was anointed by the Holy Spirit and sent to HEAL THE BROKENHEARTED and to PROCLAIM RELEASE to the captives ...those who are bound spiritually and physically.

Jesus said:

The Spirit of the LORD [is] upon Me, because He has anointed Me [the Anointed One, the Messiah] to preach the good news (the Gospel) to the poor; He has sent Me to announce release to the captives, and recovery of sight to the blind; to send forth delivered those who are oppressed [who are downtrodden, bruised, crushed and broken down by calamity].

Luke 4:18 AMP

Jesus came to proclaim RELEASE...to loose and set free those who are wounded, bruised, and bound by the past. Don't keep holding onto your hurts. This is a time of healing and restoration for the Body of Christ. His hand is stretched out to you now. Bring the deep hurts and your past to Him now and RELEASE them.

You may have tried to let go of your hurts and forget the past, but you don't know how. Somehow you still feel bound by your feelings that keep cropping up. You want to let go of the painful memories, the hurt feelings, the rejection, the anger, resentment, bitterness, and unforgiveness that has you bound, but somehow you haven't been able to.

HOW DO I RELEASE MY HURTS AND RECEIVE HEALING?

Let's look again at the example of Joseph's life. Thirteen long years, from the time he was sold into slavery until he was appointed second in command to Pharaoh, he experienced many deep hurts. In a dream, God had revealed to him how he was going to be exalted and how God was going to use him. Yet for thirteen years he experienced many disappointments, much pain, and sorrow.

Joseph was hated, rejected, and sold into slavery by his own brothers; falsely accused and slandered by Potiphar's wife; misjudged by Potiphar and thrown into prison; but he didn't become a victim bound by hatred, bitterness, resentment, or unforgiveness. He was victorious and able to draw a line on his past because he RELEASED his hurts and was healed and restored to TOTAL WHOLENESS.

During Joseph's time of trial, God was in control of his circumstances and was taking what Satan had meant for evil and was turning it around for Joseph's good. Even while he was in prison, God prospered Joseph and gave him favor. When Joseph was released from prison and was exalted to a position of great power...second in command only to Pharaoh...he married an Egyptian woman who later gave birth to two sons.

Joseph named his firstborn son Manasseh, and said:

> *It is because God has made me forget all my trouble and all my father's household.*
>
> Genesis 41:51 NIV

The Hebrew name of Manasseh is translated "God has taken the sting out of my memories." The name of his second child, Ephraim, is translated, "God has made me fruitful." Joseph was healed of his deep hurts because he RELEASES them. He harbored no bitterness, anger, or ill will whatsoever toward his brothers who had deeply hurt him. He was a victor...not a victim. He had forgiven them and RELEASED the past with its hurts, and he was healed and set free.

What was the key to his RELEASE?

FORGIVENESS! Forgiveness breaks the chains of our past. It focuses our perspective forward instead of backward on old hurts.

Joseph fully and completely forgave his brothers for the grave injustice and mistreatment he had suffered at their hands. He drew them close to himself, embraced them and wept over them. His forgiveness was not just an emotional reaction or a temporary thing. It was sincere and genuine.

FORGIVENESS is the key to RELEASE!

Forgiveness is the power to liberate us from the hurts of the past. The moment we are hurt, we have a choice...to hold onto our resentment and remain a victim, or to CHOOSE to forgive and become whole once again.

Our responsibility before God is to forgive and RELEASE the past, no matter how deeply we may have been hurt or what the other person does. It does not matter whether or not we feel like forgiving. We may have been hurt so badly we may feel we are incapable of forgiving the person who has hurt us. Even though we know we should forgive and let go of the hurts of the past, we are bound to the past by our feelings.

FORGIVENESS is not a FEELING. It is a conciliate act of our wills in obedience to God's command. Our RELEASE from our sins and the hurts of our past are dependent upon whether or not we forgive. Unless we are willing to forgive others, we cannot be forgiven.

When Jesus taught His disciples to pray, He included forgiveness as part of the prayer.

> *For if ye forgive men their trespasses, your heavenly Father will also forgive you: But if ye forgive not men their trespasses, neither will your Father forgive your trespasses.*
>
> Matthew 6:14-15

To RELEASE the past with its hurts, you must, AS AN ACT OF YOUR WILL, forgive all those who have hurt you. As you forgive them, you are being healed and RELEASED of your past with its deep hurts, sins, failures, and disappointments.

Jesus told his disciples:

> *So be merciful, sympathetic, tender, responsive and compassionateeven as your Father is (all these). Judge not, neither pronouncing judgment nor subjecting to censure and you will not be judged; do not condemn and pronounce guilty, and you will not be condemned and pronounced guilty; acquit and forgive and release (give up resentment, let it drop), and you will be acquitted and forgiven and released.*
>
> Luke 6:36-37 AMP

131

Jesus said, "Acquit and forgive and release (give up resentment, let it drop), and you will be acquitted and forgiven and released" (verse 37). In the King James Bible, this phrase is translated *"forgive, and ye shall be forgiven."* The Greek word for "forgive" is *apolou,* which means "to RELEASE...to loose from."

When we RELEASE forgiveness AS AN ACT OF OUR WILLS toward those who have gossiped, slandered, and mistreated us, WE ARE RELEASED from the past with its deep hurts. God pours in the healing oil of the Holy Spirit and restores us to WHOLENESS. He takes the pain out of our memories. And when Satan tries to stir up the past and open the wounds that have healed, we must continually REFUSE to allow him to use our past to defeat us.

AS WE RELEASE FORGIVENESS, WE ARE RELEASED FROM OUR HURTS!

God is bringing us into a new dimension of spiritual maturity where we are no longer bound by our feelings, but are moved and motivated by "Thus saith the Lord!" We are entering into a new dimension, whereby we are no longer walking in the flesh but in the Spirit...where our spirits are RULING over our souls...mind, will, emotions, and feelings...and our bodies with their physical appetites.

When we are hurt, we must no longer REACT IN THE FLESH...but ACT ACCORDING TO THE SPIRIT OF GOD that is ruling in us! When another member of the Body, our husband or wife, family member, employer, neighbor, offends or sins against us, instead of fighting back, allowing a root of bitterness to take hold, or carrying around hurt feelings; we are to RELEASE those hurts by RELEASING forgiveness.

Paul told the Colossians:

> *Therefore, as God's chosen people, holy and dearly loved, clothe yourselves with compassion, kindness, humility, gentleness and patience. Bear with each other and forgive whatever grievances you may have against one another. Forgive as the Lord forgave you. And over all these virtues put on love, which binds them all together in perfect unity.*
>
> Colossians 3:12-14 NIV

If we have grievances...disagreement with other members of the Body...we are to FORGIVE AS God HAS FORGIVEN US. Paul told the Ephesians:

> *And be ye kind to one another, tenderhearted, forgiving one another, even as God for Christ's sake hath forgiven you.*
>
> Ephesians 4:32

This is the kind of forgiveness God wants to see manifested within the Body of Christ today. We are to forgive one another according to the measure God has forgiven us. Jesus has made it very clear that, unless we are willing to forgive one another, we cannot be forgiven.

God has shown me that one of the greatest needs in the Body right now is for the Church of Jesus Christ to have a spiritual breakthrough in UNDERSTANDING, RECEIVING, AND MANIFESTING GOD'S GRACE AND FORGIVENESS.

Within the Body of Christ, we see very little of the grace of God and His forgiveness being manifested among members. Instead of extending God's grace, mercy, and FORGIVENESS to other members who have made mistakes, Christians are quick to criticize, gossip, and backbite.

Instead of FORGIVING and being reconciled to their brothers and sisters in the Lord who mistreat them, they fight back...they quarrel...they harbor resentment...they lash out in anger. Instead of taking the wrong, as the Scriptures teach, they take their brothers and sisters to court.

Instead of restoring and lifting up weaker members of the Body who have needs and faults, many Christians become self-righteous and set themselves up on a high spiritual plane. They become judgmental.

It is time for the Church to put the past with its hurts behind us...to get rid of all bitterness, anger, and unforgiveness toward other members within the Body and be healed and restored in our relationships.

When conflicts arise with other members of the Body, our goal must be RESTORATION and RECONCILIATION. Jesus told His disciples:

> *If your brother sins against you, go and show him his fault, just between the two of you. If he listens to you, you have won your brother over. But if he will not listen, take one or two others along, so that 'every matter may be established by the testimony of two or three witnesses.' If he refuses to listen to them, tell it to the church; and if he refuses to listen even to the church, treat him as you would a pagan or a tax collector.*
> Matthew 18:15-17 NIV

Too often what happens when one member of the Body is hurt by another member, instead of going to the person who has sinned against them to seek reconciliation, they talk about what happened behind the other person's back. This only causes confusion, strife, and contention within the Body.

WE MUST COME TO A PLACE OF REPENTANCE, HEALING, AND RESTORATION!

As members together of the Body of Christ, we must recognize how much we need each other. None of us is sufficient in ourselves. I am not complete without you, and you are not complete without me. We are mutually dependent upon one another. There are strengths in your life that I need, as well as strengths in my life that you need. There are strengths in your life that other members of the Body need, and strengths in their lives that you need.

If ever there was a time when we needed to lift up one another in prayer and draw strength from one another, it is now! James instructed the believers:

> *Confess to one another therefore your faults (your slips, your false steps, your offenses, your sins); and pray [also] for one another, that you may be healed and restored...*
>
> James 5:16 AMP

The time has come when we, as members of the Body of Christ, need to confess our faults one to another. I'm not suggesting that members of the Body go around indiscriminately confessing their weaknesses, faults, and sins to every member. What I am suggesting is that you go to another brother or sister in the Body...who is walking in the Spirit...who knows how to go deep into the spirit realm, locate the enemy, bind him, and win the battle.

Acknowledge your weakness, fault, or temptation that you are struggling with, the hurts you are carrying; and then join in a prayer covenant with them until the victory is won. As you covenant together in prayer for one another,

135

you will be able to draw strength from one another, and you will be healed and restored.

As the Body of Christ, we need to come to a place of repentance, healing, and restoration. We must repent before God, confess our faults to one another and covenant together in prayer for one another...lifting up one another and drawing strength from one another. As we do this, we are going to walk in greater strength than ever before.

RELEASE THE HURTS AND BE HEALED IN THE NAME OF JESUS!

This is the time of RELEASE...a time for you to let go of all deep hurts you have been carrying...to get rid of the feelings that have bound you to the past...a time for you to be healed and made 100 percent WHOLE!

Think about the past...the deep hurts you have experienced, the pain, the sorrow, and the heartache. Think about the anger, resentment, and unforgiveness you have carried in your spirit toward those who have hurt you. Think about any bitterness and rebellion that may have taken hold in your life. Think about your past sins and failures that Satan has been trying to use to hinder you from fulfilling God's destiny for your life.

Now, stretch out your hands and imagine you are holding all those things in your hands. As you are there, in the Presence of God, begin to release them one by one. By faith, see Christ unloosing the chains...the bondage of the past... and setting you free.

RELEASE...forgive all those who have hurt you in the past.

Regardless of what they have done toward you or their attitude and feelings toward you, freely forgive them. Whether it is a parent, child, husband, wife, family member, pastor, another member of the Body, friend, employer, employee...RELEASE them! Don't wait until you feel like it. Do it NOW! As an act of your will, call out their name, and tell the Lord, in obedience to His Word, that you choose to forgive them. Draw upon His dunamis strength within you.

RELEASE the burden of guilt and condemnation you have been carrying.

Satan will continue to use it against you to keep you beaten down, feeling unforgiven, unloved, and unworthy to be used of God. Don't let him torment your mind over past sins and failures. Get rid of it!

RELEASE...let go of the past with its deep hurts!

Whatever hurts you have been carrying that Satan continues to use to torment your mind...RELEASE them now. You don't have to remain a victim...bound to those who have hurt you. It's time for you to let go of them and be set free by the power of Almighty God!

RELEASE...get rid of the hurt of rejection that has been binding you!

Rejection is one of the worst, most neglected, and most common wounds. You may feel rejection from your husband or wife, from family members, from people in your church, or those you work with. You may carry deep wounds where you feel unloved, unaccepted, and unwanted. You may feel unlovable and may feel incapable of loving others. RELEASE those

137

wounds NOW! You are loved, forgiven, and accepted by the King of kings and Lord of lords!

RELEASE...all bitterness and any root of rebellion that may have taken root in your life.

Bitterness will not only torment your mind and block your healing...Satan will try to use it to destroy you. He wants you to remain in bitterness so that you will be spiritually paralyzed. Don't even allow a trace of it to remain. RELEASE it now... PLUCK IT OUT BY THE ROOT in the Name of Jesus.

Beloved, draw a line on your past. Let me know you are drawing a line on your past by filling out the coupon on the last page of this book. I will lay hands on the form to release God's healing into your life for your deepest hurts!

After you have RELEASED all these things, lift your hands to the Father, right where you are.

RECEIVE HEALING AND RESTORATION!

RECEIVE NEW STRENGTH!

RECEIVE HEALING FOR YOUR SOUL...mind...will... emotions...feelings!

RECEIVE HEALING FOR YOUR BODY!

Jesus came to PROCLAIM RELEASE TO THE CAPTIVES...to SET FREE THOSE WHO ARE BRUISED! BE RELEASED from your hurts! BE RELEASED from your painful memories! BE RELEASED and MADE WHOLE in the Name of Jesus!

Say aloud: "God has planned for me to experience TOTAL WHOLENESS...spirit...soul...body...where I am continually being healed, continually being restored, continually being strengthened by His Spirit living within me!"

Now turn to the back page of this book and prepare to take the next step.

Faith is a fact, but faith is an act. Turn to the special response coupon on the back page of this book to receive your FREE copy of my audiotape, *"Turning Your Sorrows Into 100% Victory,"* and my book, *Divine Appointment With Destiny,* for this very hour!

In these last few moments before the return of Jesus Christ, we, as a Church, must move on from where we are and go where God is leading us!

This incredible new book and audiotape will encourage you and lead you into your end-time destiny!

...and God gave me a vision!

There is a greater anointing upon me now than ever before to pray for your needs.

Never before, in my more than 58 years of frontline ministry have I carried a deeper burden for the Body of Christ than I do now. I have prayed, fasted, interceded, agonized, and fought spiritual warfare against satanic powers...

...and God gave me a vision!

A vision of Jesus Christ, our Great High Priest, praying for all your needs.

God said, *"Place the needs of my people upon the altar before My Presence. Jesus is praying for all their needs to be met."*

Every need, every disease, every family problem, every circumstance... God wants me to lift your need for Jesus to pray for you. Do not delay. Write all your needs on the following page and mail it to me today!

For prayer call:

1-858-435-7546

Brother Cerullo,

Please place these requests on the Miracle Prayer Altar and pray for these needs:

_____

_____

_____

_____

_____

❑ Enclosed is my love gift of $(£)_____ to help you win souls and to support this worldwide ministry.

❑ Please tell me how I can become a God's Victorious Army member...to help you reach the nations of the world and receive even more anointed teaching on a monthly basis!

Name _____

Address _____

City _____ State or Province _____

Postal Code _____ Phone Number ( ) _____

E-mail _____

Fax _____

Mail today to:

MORRIS CERULLO WORLD EVANGELISM
San Diego: P.O. Box 85277 • San Diego, CA 92186
Canada: P.O. Box 3600 • Concord, Ontario L4K 1B6
U.K.: P.O. Box 277 • Hemel Hempstead, Herts HP2 7DH
Web site: www.mcwe.com • E-mail: morriscerullo@mcwe.com

For prayer, call: 1-858-435-7546

PRAYER LINE FAX: 1-858-427-0555

PRAYER LINE E-MAIL: prayer@mcwe.com

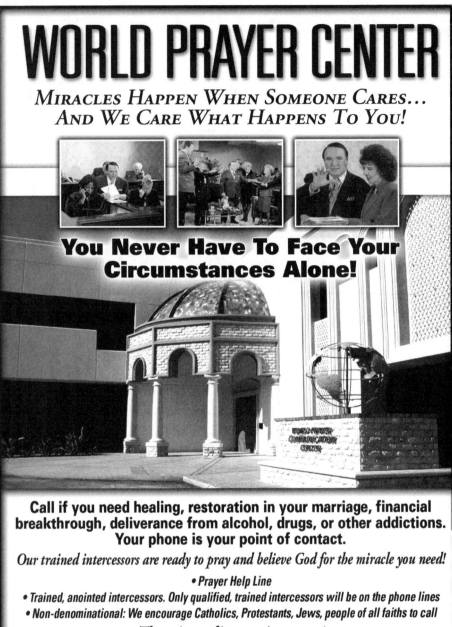

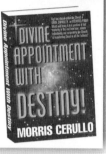

Published by:
MORRIS CERULLO WORLD EVANGELISM
First Printing 1998
Second Printing 2002
Third Printing 2005
Fourth Printing 2006
P.O. Box 85277 • San Diego, CA 92186
(858) 277-2200
E-mail: morriscerullo@mcwe.com

Website: www.mcwe.com

For prayer, call: (858)HELPLINE
435-7546
E-mail: HELPLINE@mcwe.com

MORRIS CERULLO WORLD EVANGELISM OF CANADA
P.O. Box 3600 • Concord, Ontario L4K-1B6
(905) 669-1788

MORRIS CERULLO WORLD EVANGELISM OF GREAT BRITAIN
P.O. Box 277 • Hemel Hempstead, HERTS HP2-7DH
+(0)1 442 232432

GOD'S ANSWERS
To Heal Your
Deep Hurts

How To Overcome The World And Live
Without The Pain And Fears Of The Past

Morris Cerullo